THE SMALL BUDGET
GARDENER

Published by Cool Springs Press
P.O. Box 2828
Brentwood, TN 37024

Cataloging-in-Publication data available

EAN 978-1-59186-461-5

First Printing, Revised Edition 2009

Printed in the United States of America
10 9 8 7 6 5 4 3 2 1

Editor: Billie Brownell
Design: Bill Kersey, Kersey Graphics
Cover Design: Marc Pewitt

PHOTOGRAPHY
Artville: 80
Cathy Wilkinson Barash: 162
Paula Biles: 160
Ferry-Morse: 167
Fiskars: 17, 111
Maureen Gilmer: 10, 11, 13, 14, 15, 16, 23, 24, 26, 27, 28, 34, 36, 37 top,
38, 40, 43, 46, 47, 54, 55 top, 58, 62, 65, 69, 71, 72, 74, 76, 85, 86, 87, 88,
89, 91, 02 top, 104 top, 110, 112, 113, 114, 116, 117, 118, 120, 122, 123,
125, 126, 127, 129, 130, 131, 132, 134, 135, 136, 138, 139, 140, 141, 142,
143, 144, 145, 147, 148, 149, 151, 152, top left, 152 bottom, 153, 154,
157, 159, 166, 175, 176, 177, 178, 182, 183, 184, 186, 187, 188, 189, 191,
192, 193, 200, 202, 204, 205, 206, 207, 208, 210, 213, 214, 215, 216, 218,
219 bottom, 221, 223, 224, 225, 226, 227, 228, 230, 231
Jupiter Images: 8, 52, 53, 59, 84, 88, 90, 164, 174, 212
Jessie Keith 98, 100, 102 bottom, 103, 104 bottom
Joe Lamp'l: 20
Neil Soderstrom: 37 bottom, 46, 48
Charles Mann: 55 bottom
Mark A. Miller: 219 top
Felder Rushing: 146, 152 top right
Courtenay Vanderbilt, 68, 92

Visit the Cool Springs Press website at www.coolspringspress.com

THE SMALL BUDGET
GARDENER

MAUREEN GILMER

COOL SPRINGS PRESS

Growing Successful Gardeners™
www.coolspringspress.com
BRENTWOOD, TENNESSEE

Introduction

What goes around, comes around. You can prove this saying by checking the economic history of the United States with its recurring cycles of boom and bust, prosperity and recession. This is not the first time we have experienced hard times as a nation, and we can meet the challenges head-on with old-fashioned Yankee ingenuity and a new appreciation for the wealth of the garden. It's just the first time many younger Americans with families are seeing mass layoffs and zero growth.

We can look back as recently as the 1970s to see how Americans coped with an absence of cash and a dim employment picture. Back then we had the same factors: an unpopular war, sky-high energy prices, layoffs, and mortgage woes. And there is another parallel to these two ages—Americans are waking up to a threatened environment. Back then the ecology movement was born; today it's global warming and the green revolution.

No wonder clothing styles are going back to those of the '60s counterculture. We're living history over again. With little money to travel or pay for luxuries, everyone is turning to their own backyard to find solutions. Back then the fix was to "Grow your own," while today the goals are not only to grow your own food but to find a rewarding lifestyle at home in your garden.

Hard times can be good times if we return to the garden for all the beauty, health, and comfort it can provide. Rather than dwelling on what we don't have, gardening reminds us of just how much one can grow for next to nothing. Plus, discovering inexpensive or free alternatives to goods we have purchased in the past makes it possible to grow and create far more than you ever imagined. Think of budget gardening as a giant scavenger hunt where you can discover hidden treasures in the unlikeliest places. Some of these discoveries will be old ideas turned new again. Others will be inspired by the movement to recycle and live "greener" to benefit the environment. And still more will come out of your own imagination, with brilliant ideas for great designs, one-of-a-kind accents, and cultivation of unusual plants.

Perhaps your budget garden will become your best garden ever because it won't be one you buy—it will be one you create.

Table of Contents

PART ONE

Stretch Every Dollar

Getting money is like digging with a needle; spending it is like water soaking into sand. – Japanese Proverb

AT MY HOME IN THE MOUNTAINS WE LIVED ON A SHOESTRING.
It was thirty miles from a small town, so anytime I needed anything it was a very long drive, not to mention the cost of gas. During those years when this book was in its formative stages, I learned just how little I needed to get by. Sometimes it was many days between the time I needed something and the time I could go to town to pick it up. This gave me time to think about whether I really needed it. And often those interim days became productive when I found an alternate way of getting the job done without spending a penny. Finding alternatives became my primary practice; not only saving me the time and gas to go to town but also the money I would have spent on the item's purchase price.

This part of the book is designed to help you start thinking as though you live thirty miles from town. Then, when you do shop, you will better know what to buy and what to pass by. Chapter 1 helps a new gardener learn what's gimmicky and what's really useful so you'll only buy what you need. Chapter 2 details how to get more plants for your dollar through some practical and ingenious shopping tips. Chapter 3 looks at how to get your soil in shape for free, or nearly so.

For every gardener, not just those on a tight budget, these chapters can jump-start your gardening efforts while helping you spend as little money as possible. You'll discover the joy of an abundant harvest of delicious organic food for a one-time investment in tools. Every day will become a rainbow of color when your beautiful landscape blooms from once small, modestly priced seedlings. And best of all, you can dabble in the soil and expect great success, no matter how empty your bank account.

1 Buy It Right and Buy It Once:
Essentials yes, junk no.

Always ask yourself, "Do I want that thing, or do I need it?"
If it's a need, then buy it. If it's a want, then walk away.

One of my pet peeves is how gardening is portrayed on TV and the way that influences how we create gardens. Advertisements of gimmicky tools create one of the primary money wasters because these are sold as the ultimate problem solvers. But what many new gardeners don't realize is that the soil in the ads doesn't resemble typical garden soil at all, nor do the weeds in the demo cling to earth as tenaciously as those in our yards. Too often these gimmick tools end up abandoned in the garage when they fail to function in the real world as they do on TV. And the price for that item, plus the shipping and handling costs, is lost forever.

The real problem is to know exactly what you need and what you can live without. That's no easy matter when you're faced with a staggering array of items at a home improvement store. It gets even worse when you're catalog shopping. One of America's oldest landscape suppliers is A.M. Leonard, a catalog retailer that offers more than thirty-six kinds of shovels, twenty-eight rakes, and eighteen hoes! It's no wonder home gardeners are taken in by the sales pitch for the quintessential labor-saving gimmick. It's a lot easier to buy that do-it-all item when you're overwhelmed by this very great array of choices. I understand because the more choices I have, the more difficult it is for me to choose. I learned this in restaurants; large, varied menus leave me unable to make a meal choice, but when I go to McDonalds I have no trouble choosing a hamburger! In this ever more diverse world complicated by online shopping, I know you're just as stymied.

When there are so many brands and prices, pay attention to the details of any tool you buy.

Hand Tools

I've spent more than thirty years growing things and I have very specific preferences when it comes to hand tools. Being a tightwad, I make my tools last a long time and I'm unlikely to add anything to my basic list this late in the game. Being a generalist in the garden, I grow all sorts of plants, and this list is a result of that kind of

Basic Hand Tools and Why You Need Them

Many of these tools are manufactured with either a long handle or a short handle with a D-grip. Test both to determine which is best for that type of tool and the work it will do in the garden.

Pointed shovel Used for: *Digging holes; turning soil.*
Fiberglass handles are lighter weight for the not-so-strong users. Look for a heavy metal blade, particularly if you live where there is clay or rocky ground that can snap or crack a handle under very little pressure.

Flat shovel Used for: *Scraping hard surfaces like concrete; scooping soil and additives; clean up.*
Choose a heavier steel shovel for longevity. Lightweight aluminum types designed for snow are better for the not-so-strong users or when dealing with lightweight materials such as leaves.

Narrow spade Used for: *Digging trenches or small holes for container plants.*
This shovel is most useful if the blade is about the size of a one-gallon plant. It makes very little mess by digging a perfectly sized hole or digging in a confined space. It's also useful for the digging necessary for the repair or expansion of sprinkler systems.

Spading fork Used for: *Digging up plants without damaging roots; turning soil.*
This is the essential tool for every gardener to lift perennials and transplant with minimal root damage. When turning heavy soil, a spading fork requires a lot less work and doesn't cause clay to compact in the process.

Hoe Used for: *Chopping weeds; fashioning rows for vegetables; cleaning narrow crevices.*
Blade quality of a hoe is paramount. Good steel allows you to sharpen it with a file so it melts through weeds like butter rather than forcing you to hack away all day with a dull edge. Pay close attention to how well the head is attached to the handle, as this is vital to how long it lasts.

Hand trowel Used for: *Digging small holes for annuals, perennials, or seeds; planting container plants.*
Choose one that is strong and feels good in your hand. Those cast from a single piece of aluminum are lightweight, strong, and nearly indestructible. Those with many connected parts, such as a separate handle and shaft, too often come apart.

Planting axe Used for: *Quickly digging small holes for small container and bedding plants.*
This little known but highly useful landscaper's tool places far less pressure on the wrist than using a hand trowel for planting in undisturbed ground. One that's well balanced with a heavy head gives you better leverage. Properly weighted axes help you do a lot more while exerting substantially less energy than the super lightweight types.

Small leaf rake Used for: *Removing leaves and trash from between or under plants.*
Small leaf rakes that become an extension of your arm can be a real problem solver for small gardens where spaces are tight.

Large leaf rake Used for: *Raking leaves and other lightweight materials.*
The wide range of sizes and materials, from real bamboo to plastic, result in a lightweight tool that can cover a great deal of ground in a short time.

Bow iron rake Used for: *Raking heavy materials and leveling the ground; preparing to plant.*
The bow iron rake is key to moving and leveling soil, and it is one of the most often used tools in areas of rocky ground as you cull the clods and pebbles to yield a clean, finely leveled surface for a project or for planting.

Wheelbarrow Used for: *Carrying heavy loads, particularly on narrow pathways.*

Despite all the newfangled two-wheel garden carts, the one-wheel wheelbarrow remains unmatched for agility and ease of use both for light- and heavyweight loads. Know any gate dimensions before buying a wide load model to ensure it fits through the gate easily.

Hand clippers Used for: *Pruning smaller soft and hard materials.*

This is the most personal of tools because it's used to prune everything from fresh flowers to tree branches. Choose one that fits your hand and has quality blades that you can sharpen for years to come; it is a bargain at any price.

Loppers Used for: *Pruning larger branches and roots.* Long-handled loppers extend your reach and expand your cutting ability. Weight can be a big issue, particularly for women, so be sure to select the perfect balance between the strength of the product and how much it weighs.

Pruning saw Used for: *Removing large limbs and roots too thick to cut with loppers.*

Essential for pruning trees and shrubs with larger limbs, or for anything too large to cut with loppers.

Long-handled bulb planter Used for: *Creating perfectly cylindrical holes for bulbs.*

The long-handled form is a bit more costly but it saves your wrist from damage when planting more than a few bulbs, and it's a great way to dig holes for vegetable seedlings.

Good shovels, flat or pointed, should be made of high-quality steel and a strong handle so they won't bend or crack under pressure.

diversity. However, if you decide to specialize in one kind of plant such as roses or citrus trees, then you may want a few additional items unique to that specialty. But in general, if you acquire these tools, you will always have the right one for practically any job that comes along.

Tired of Running For Tools All The Time?

One of the few truly innovative tools is this all-purpose tool that folds up neatly to fit in your pocket so you can snip or repair anything at the spur of the moment.

Pocket Boy® saws are another small but very useful tool that fits nicely into a back pocket where it's ready when you need it.

Love, Hate, and the "Quality" Garden Hose

Though it is not technically a tool, the garden hose is the most often used item in the garden. It can also be the most frustrating part of your gardening experience if the hose is old, in bad repair, or not well made in the first place. The truth is that poorly made hoses make it a hassle to water, and that means you may be less inclined to water as often as you should. The result could be a garden that languishes, and your investment in time and money is lost. Therefore, making a wise investment in good quality hoses will maximize every penny you spend on your plants.

Typically, poor-quality hoses kink at the slightest tug, or thin metal couplings fail to cross-thread. For those who live in the Sunbelt, UV degradation of the plastics and rubber used to make garden hoses can severely reduce its lifespan. Buying a good-quality garden hose that is UV resistant and well made is a good investment as it should last for many years of service. Buying on the cheap is the fast track to kinks and leaking couplers and splits,

Shopping Guidelines

Retailers know that gardeners, like every other kind of shopper, are vulnerable to impulse buying. After all, that's how the Garden Weasel was sold, because it certainly did not become popular by word of mouth! Crafty retailers know exactly how to entice you to buy more than you planned, buy a different product than you came for, and choose the brand with the largest profit margin for the store. Become a savvy consumer in the garden center. Not only will you save those impulse-buy dollars, you'll come home with exactly what you need to get the job done.

Always make a list. Just as with supermarket shopping, making a list of exactly what you need to buy is your best insurance against overspending or buying things you really don't need.

Inspect wood handles. With so many tools now imported, the quality of the wood used can be highly variable. Poor-quality wood can warp, crack, and shrink in transit, resulting in a vastly weaker handle. Inspect the handle to ensure it's made of solid, heavyweight wood that is free of flaws. Check the connection to the metal head because wood handles can shrink in shipping and become loose by the time they reach a retailer. Since it's an old-time tradition to replace handles of gardening tools when they become aged, be sure your new choice offers that option. Many don't, so if they can't be replaced, your only hope is to transform it into garden art.

Beware of weak or metal prongs. Whether they are on a cultivating claw, a spading fork, or a bow rake, strong prongs won't bend out of shape or break under pressure. Using these tools in typical clay or rocky soils can break a tine in no time. This is doubly true for a spading fork, the most useful and versatile tool you can have. A thick tine fork is essential.

Avoid overly thin blades. This is an affliction of the global marketplace. A thin-bladed shovel will not hold up under pressure, and if you have heavy soil you absolutely need the strongest blade you can get. Even a smaller woman is strong enough to bend a shovel blade in clay soil, and if you have to baby your shovel you won't get much work done. A heavy blade can also be sharpened with a grinder or a flat file. A well-honed hoe blade is so much easier to use it cuts the work load in half. Poor steel or overly thin steel not only resists a sharp edge, it gets dull again after very little use.

Watch out for loose connections. While this subject has been covered a bit already, connections can also be metal to metal. This is where overseas manufacturing produces a galaxy of low-cost tools that just don't hold up under rigorous use. These can be really poorly made tools and yet they look just like the better made ones.

This older metal rake lost its handle a long time ago and became garden art.

The many brands, thicknesses, and lengths can make buying a hose confusing. The best buy, as always, is found by comparing price to longevity in your local climate.

which all result in the expense of buying a replacement hose.

Avoid gimmick hoses such as the tight coil spring form sold on TV. What they don't show you is now easily the hoses kink into a snarl, or that the hose's tension is tugging all the time so you can't lay it down to answer the phone without it recoiling again. Stick with well-known manufacturers that stand behind their products.

The Eternal Battle of Quality Versus Price

One thing that never changes is the price of quality, and that's the foundation of brand allegiance. In short, this means longevity and reliability over the long term. When you evaluate the various brands of tools at the store, you'll naturally go for the least expensive one because that's human nature. It will probably look identical to the quality tool, too. But to understand the real value, just do a bit of math. Calculate the price of the less expensive one; then, add that to the price of the more expensive, quality tool. Why? Because if you can't afford to buy it right, you'd better be prepared to buy it twice.

You can't judge a book by its cover, and this is true when it comes to hand tools. Bright paint and shiny metal have very little to do with quality.

Tightwad Gardening Tip

While it is not a rule, it is my observation that tools made in America and Germany tend to be of the highest quality, as are some Japanese-made brands. Those manufactured in Chinese steel plants can be of good quality too, but they are imported in such massive quantities without any discernable brand that there is no way to determine if you have a good one or not. I test a wide range of tools by using them myself or putting them to work with a couple of big strong guys I know. They apply the "Can you break it?" test. Such was the case for Wolff garden loppers from Germany. They were so lightweight we were sure they were junk; but after the "Can you break it?" test, we were convinced they are indeed a good buy.

Sometimes the only guideline you have is a known brand. Wise old gardeners will tell you that extremes of anything are to be avoided, and I agree. My philosophy is that the most expensive is too costly and the least expensive is junk, and the optimal choice will be somewhere in the middle. So put on your hunter-gatherer hat when you shop for tools. Visit a retailer that carries many different lines of tools. That's the only way you'll get a good sense of the range of prices and quality at one location, which is the key to finding the optimal middle ground.

Not-So-New Tools

For young families who rent or perhaps who are pinching pennies in order to afford their first home, there are alternatives to buying retail. Buying used is a great way to pick up your first tools for next to nothing, and the list on pages 12–13 will help you know exactly what to look for. My best treasures have been found at estate sales, but garage sales are just as promising for a good find. Estate sales stand out because these are liquidating the estate of someone who may have passed away and often has a lifetime's accumulation of gardening tools and equipment. It's not uncommon to find everything from lawn mowers to pruning shears at rock-bottom prices.

Neighborhoods that are close to military bases or colleges, or where whole industries are dying out, will be areas where many people are relocating. Second best are resort areas in warm climates where older folks retire. Palm Springs, where I live, is one of the best places for estate sales and thrift store finds in the world!

Green Choices

Estate sales are *the* places to find a vintage, manually pushed reel-type lawn mower. Older folks once used these exclusively and they are often found stored in a garage when someone moves or passes away. These old push mowers are fantastic machines that you can restore and have sharpened to clip the lawn without using gas (and breathing gas exhaust!) or electricity. *And* you can mow at any time of the day or night without waking up the neighborhood!

New push mowers using modern composites, like this one from Fiskars, are much more lightweight and easier to handle than the older, all-steel ones.

Repair It ... Don't Replace It

We have become a disposable society, with taking care of things and maintenance proving to be somewhat of a lost art. But hard economic times are forcing us to rethink the way we live. Early American farmers could survive on so little because they treasured their tools and equipment. They spent the winter repairing and rehabilitating their equipment for the coming planting season; a rusted blade or a frozen pivot bolt could cost them a whole year's crop. Metal tools will last a lifetime if they're treated properly, and you can rehabilitate a garage sale find to nearly new condition with just a little time and attention.

One of the most important tools that few homeowners possess is a flat file. This is about the size of a large wooden ruler and has a coarse texture on one side (that is coarser than the other side). A file does a dozen different jobs from shaving rust off a flat surface to honing a blade. Another good maintenance tool is a knife sharpener. The type that consists of a groove through which you slide a blade is ideal for loppers and clippers. But if a blade has a gouge in it, you'll need a flat file to smooth it out first, then sharpen it. Since few folks know how to care for tools anymore, the following paragraph describes the age-old practices of farmers who worked hard to keep their tools in working shape for decades.

Use a flat, or an electrical grinder to sharpen the edges of hoe blades and shovels. Use coarse sandpaper to sand off accumulations of rust before the rust becomes deep enough to weaken the steel. Paint the cleaned steel parts with rust-resistant paint such as Rust-Oleum. If you paint tools a bright color such as red or orange they will be easier to find if you set them down in the garden. Replace wood handles that are cracked or broken. If any damage is borderline, protect the palms of your hands by sanding the surfaces of the handle smooth, and then wrap the handle in friction tape to prevent it from pinching while in use. Oil any wood handles or paint them with weatherproof outdoor latex paint in bright colors. Tighten any loose connections. Use heavy wire, bolts, and wood screws as needed. Oil all moving parts: hinges, wheels, and so forth. Lubricate with WD-40® or 3-in-One® oil or a similar product. Sharpen cutting blades with a whetstone or a more modern knife-sharpening device. You can also send blades to be professionally sharpened, particularly when it comes to pole- or hand-pruners and loppers. Replace all bent blades because these will not cut cleanly, no matter how much you sharpen them. Store all tools in a dry place for winter and keep them shaded and out of the rain in summer.

Power Tools

Buying hand tools is fairly simple, but when confronted with power tools, even well-seasoned gardeners can be overwhelmed by the materials, features, and restrictions on newly made products. This becomes even more crucial if you strive for a green household because gasoline engines are not beneficial to the environment. Electric tools are suitable substitutes, but you will be forever tethered to a cord. Battery operated forms solve the cord problems, but these are afflicted by a short battery life and limited power.

Gas-fired engines are still the primary form of lawn mower used in America. How-to manuals for these beasts require a fundamental knowledge of mechanics, not to mention the assortment of tools you need to do the job. And it seems no matter how much we study the owner's manual, adjusting a carburetor is still a no-win situation. For as we all know, the equipment will run perfectly at the mechanic's shop, but as soon as it touches earth on the old homestead it will start spitting and smoking again, or just die.

Green Choices

Nearly every American household has a lawn and we spend *billions* each year watering, feeding, and mowing them. While a lawn makes a superior play surface, it may not be worth the cost and effort needed to maintain one that's rarely used. If you have a small lawn, ask yourself whether it might be better turned into a flower garden or vegetable plot that frees you from the weekend lawncare tasks. In the process, it will free the environment from the impact of manufactured lawn fertilizers, herbicides, and pesticides as well as excess water consumption.

This problem is not about to go away. Rather than continue the struggle, consider a reel push mower if you have a small, fairly level lawn. These are the same mowers that did the job for homeowners decades before power mowers became widely available. The new reel mowers are nearly silent, emit no pollutants, and require no gas or small engine maintenance. They cut the lawn with a clean scissor action driven by gears that make

the job easier in much the same way gears on a bicycle make it easier to pedal uphill.

For large lawns, or those too steep for a reel mower, power equipment is still the only realistic way to cut the grass. The power lawn mower has always been the single most important lawn care tool for homeowners. Today, there are dozens of different makes and models that make your choice of an economical machine difficult. But like hand tools, paying a bit more for a known brand with a solid track record is still recommended.

The best source of evaluation has always been the folks at *Consumer Reports*. Fortunately, they have gone online so their buying guides are quicker and easier to consult than ever before. Online data allows them to upgrade their evaluations at any time, so you are sure to find the latest and greatest lawn mowers reviewed on the site. This is a subscription website but it's well worth the cost as it covers just about everything a consumer might buy. Locate them at www.ConsumerReports.com.

You may have heard the acronym KISS, which means "keep it simple, stupid," and oh, how important that is! It's best illustrated by cars. A Chevy, even models as late as the 1960s, featured a simple engine and few options making them easy to diagnose and repair. Today's Chevys are rife with elaborate features that turn the engine compartment into a mass of tubes, wires, and computerized devices. There's no way you can work on your own car anymore and the same goes for many lawn mowers. Between emissions control and special features, these power tools can become downright complicated. And they've gotten a lot more expensive to diagnose and repair. The best solution is to select one that is as simple as possible from day one to save on the purchase price and ensure it can be easily repaired for many years to come.

There are other power tools that can be as indispensable as the lawn mower depending on the kind of landscape you have. Lawns should be neatly edged if they are to appear tidy, and in the past you had to buy a special edging tool to get the job done. Today's string trimmers are now far more useful if they are equipped with edging capability that makes them the power tool *du jour*. These can be powered by either a small gas engine

Homes with extensive hedges or topiary will benefit from a versatile power shear to keep their forms crisp and clean.

or electricity. For a small lawn, an electric model is simpler to operate, less polluting, quiet, and easy to start. The beauty of the string trimmer is that it can double as a weed control device, giving you two tools in one.

Anyone who plants a vegetable garden each year knows how indispensable a rototiller can be. This device is an essential tool that not only turns under the remnants of last year's crop, it helps break open soil and integrate new soil amendments for the coming year. Tillers vary in size and power, with each one designed for specific conditions. Knowing how much power you need for your type of soil and size of garden have a lot to do with the kind of tiller you should choose. If the soil is soft, sandy loam, virtually any tiller will work satisfactorily. But if you are not a physically strong person, rear tine tillers prove to be the easiest to use.

Problems can arise where soils are heavy clay, and if there are many medium to large rocks mixed into the soil. This requires a much heftier machine. Rocks take their toll both on the tines themselves and the transmission. While a tine is not easy to replace (although it can be done), a damaged transmission can be the end of that machine or the start of an expensive repair process. For this kind of problem soil it is best to buy the largest, strongest machine you can find. Those with the tines in front of the engine are also recommended because they bump over large underground boulders or heavy roots more easily than a rear tine design. Remember that the high cost of a tiller can double when the inexpensive choice proves unable to get the job done. (Note: tillers can also be rented.)

For gardens with extensive hedges or topiary, the laborious task of hand shearing makes a power hedge clipper worth its weight in gold. Though more expensive than old-fashioned hand tools, a power hedge clipper not only saves time but does a cleaner, faster job overall. This is one of the most common power tools to crop up at garage and estate sales because they are almost always electric and rarely break down. However, some new electric clipper designs feature unique types of circular blades that are much safer and reduce the risk of cutting the cord.

For homesites on forested land or where there are lots of older shade trees on the property, there is a frequent need to prune larger limbs or cut up fallen ones. Though this can be

done with a manual pruning saw, a chainsaw does the job quickly with less effort. Small gas-powered chainsaws are ideal, but to avoid polluting engines consider an electric alternative. These are easy to use and help one recycle cut limbs into firewood.

Before you invest in any other large equipment for the lawn or garden, consider the cost-benefit analysis. This compares how often you'd use a tool compared to how much you must invest to buy it. For example, you may use a wood chipper just once a year during pruning season, which doesn't justify the thousands you'd pay to own one. And, this kind of tool can be rented for a fraction of the purchase price. Better yet, the folks at the rental yard must store, repair, and maintain it, so you can be sure it will start and run properly when the time comes. A chipper that sits for most of the year must be drained and properly stored or it will become difficult to start, particularly with the new gasoline formulations that can result in sludge in the carburetor.

The array of plant care products is mindboggling and you can easily waste money if you don't shop smart.

Garden Products Galore

The garden department of a home improvement store or garden center features a staggering array of products designed for plant care. Bottles, bags, and boxes are packaged just like supermarket goods to catch your eye with bright colors and bold graphics. But if you look closely at the labels, you'll find the vast majority can be categorized either as a fertilizer, pest-control product, or herbicide. And just like supermarket products, there are name brands—and their generic counterparts that sell for less.

Fertilizer from the fishing industry includes kelp, which gives a special kick for improved plant growth.

Generics can be a great way to save money in your garden. Closely inspect the ingredient labels just as you do food products to compare their contents. All fertilizers are labeled with three numbers (NPK) that explain the relative amounts of nitrogen, phosphorus, and potassium—the basic nutrients plants need. The NPK are expressed as percentages of the product, such as 10-10-10 (10 percent nitrogen, 10 percent phosphorus, and 10 percent potassium). These numbers are key to accurate comparison shopping.

For example, assume a special rose fertilizer in its fancy packaging and small, impulse-buy size is displayed at eye level on a shelf. It sells for about $7 for 2 pounds and is labeled 20-15-10, meaning it contains 20 percent nitrogen, 15 percent phosphorous, and 10 percent potassium. There might be a trace of sulfur or iron in there too, whether your soil needs it or not. This works out to about $3.50 per pound of product.

Now, look at the larger bags of granular fertilizer that are sometimes stored at the base of a shelf or even outdoors away from the smaller, more costly products on the shelves. Look at the formula label on each bag to find one that is close to the same percentages as that costly rose food. You might find something similar, such as 23-16-8, priced at $10 for a 20-pound bag. Sure, it isn't labeled with fancy colors, nor does it say "Rose Food" on the bag, yet its contents are nearly identical to the special formula for roses. At its price you're paying just 50 cents per pound!

It doesn't take a rocket scientist to see the difference in price for virtually the same product. Any experienced rose aficionado will tell you that roses are heavy feeders and a two-pound box won't last very long. If you could look into his or her garden shed, you're likely to find the generic there, probably in a 50-pound bag!

Frugal Fertilizers
Green Choices

(Strict organic gardeners can skip this section and refer to the soil improvers detailed in Chapter 2.) Because fertilizers speed plant growth and compensate for poor soil, they are the most widely used garden products. Unlike chemical pest- and weed-control products, which are used sporadically, fertilizer must be applied regularly throughout the growing season for best results.

By and large, most homeowners use synthetic fertilizers that are basically plant nutrients created in a pure and easy-to-use form. These are sold in four forms: dry granules, water-soluble crystals, liquid concentrates, and slow-release concentrated stakes. You'll also find various types of compressed pellets and other unique forms of slow-release fertilizers for less needy plants such as wildflowers, western natives, and cacti.

Dry granules are the most commonly used because they are cheap, easy to package, and even easier to apply. These are largely lawn fertilizers, which have undergone great changes in the last decades. Here, too, the name brands will cost more than their generic equivalents provided their nutrient content is roughly the same. Formulas can also be specific to certain

Tightwad Gardening Tip

Some lawn fertilizers contain herbicides that selectively kill certain kinds of weeds while helping to maintain a healthy lawn. Such high-tech formulas cost more because they include more than just nutrients. Before you count them out, factor in your real-time costs and what that is worth. How much time will it take to hand weed the lawn or how much will it cost to pay someone else to do it? For those with a busy lifestyle and where lawns are large and high profile, the additional cost of such multipurpose fertilizers is well worth it.

Each time you water, time-release fertilizer dissolves a bit more to provide consistent plant nutrition for up to three months at a time.

types of grass because Bermuda, for example, is not as demanding as bluegrass.

Water-soluble crystals became famous through the national advertising campaign of Miracle Gro®, which has evolved into a huge line of fertilizer products. The beauty of one of their topselling products is that it is applied through a hose-end applicator gun that automatically blends fertilizer with water so you feed while you water the garden. This ease of use is a big reason why it's so popular, but you may end up using more than you need because once you fill the applicator reservoir with product, you cannot save the excess for next time. You must apply it all or discard the leftover product, which presents a new problem: where to dump all that nitrogen without threatening the environment.

While Miracle Gro® is the most well known, there are other brands such as Peter's that have similar formulas and applicator guns. Over the long term, this lower price can be a big benefit, so check prices to ensure you're getting a good deal before choosing the name brand.

In the past, liquid fertilizer concentrate, both synthetic and organic in origin, was mixed in a watering can and applied, which limited its popularity. Many of these, such as fish emulsion, were too thick to be applied through a hose-end applicator gun. Recently, Miracle Gro® expanded its line to include a liquid concentrate form of its traditional formula. It's sold in bottles just like soda pop that you screw onto a hose-end applicator. This is much more economical because if there is leftover concentrate you simply unscrew the bottle from the applicator gun and replace the cap. It can be stored for the next time without wasting a drop.

Green Choices

Fish emulsion, a brown, soupy byproduct of the fishing industry, has long been the most widely used liquid concentrate fertilizer. It is organic and gardeners have found it is quite effective on food plants, making this one of the old-time gardener's most trusted plant foods. Scientists finally looked into this product to see why it is such a successful fertilizer because technically, it wasn't that potent. What they found was kelp, which is found in fish emulsion, contains certain chemicals that stimulate cell division in plants. Fish emulsion,

Tightwad Gardening Tip

Spray Safe. When you must spray a plant to apply a pest-control product, it's important to know the time of day when the job is best accomplished. If you spray when it's sunny, the spray will sit on the leaves where the sun's rays become intensified just as they would if you used a magnifying glass. This exposure can result in widespread leaf damage, which is even greater when using oil sprays. The best time to apply these materials is in the evening so it can sit on the leaves all night and do its job before evaporating in the morning. If you want to limit the time a product is on the leaves, spray very early in the morning before sunrise to allow the maximum amount of time before the sun shines on the leaves. Be sure to spray both tops and bottoms of the leaves where insects often hide. The same applies to fungus diseases, which may linger in the cool, shady undersides of the leaves.

This fuzzy white fluff on prickly pear cactus is a scale insect known as cochineal, which hides under its soft cloak to suck juices out of the plant. It can be controlled with jets of water to wash them off, but they will return. But if a plant is washed clean and then an insecticidal soap product is applied, cochineal scale is far less likely to return.

therefore, is more than just a great green fertilizer; it also offers a natural steroid that makes your plants bigger and better.

Time-release fertilizers have been in demand because they are slowly released and reduce the frequency of application. Plant stakes are one way to solve this problem, but they tend to concentrate too heavily in one small spot when you need a product that releases nutrition over the entire root zone. For decades the nursery industry has used a product called Osmocote®, which is a unique slow-release fertilizer. Its form is one of tiny, BB-sized balls encased in an outer covering that allows the fertilizer inside to slowly dissolve into the soil. It's excellent for container plants because each time the plants are watered the pellet dissolves a tiny bit, ensuring there is a continuous supply of nutrients. Here,

African marigolds are rather large annual flowers at maturity, growing to well over knee high. To make them better suited to smaller gardens, breeders have produced dwarf forms, which make it possible to add this useful plant to size-challenged food gardens.

too, Miracle Gro® has created its own slow-release pellets, but many generics are in a slow-release form. Slow-release products are more expensive but are an economical choice for small yards and homeowners who don't have time to feed very often. However, for heavy feeders like roses or annual flowers, this won't be enough, so plan on including the cost of more potent fertilizers to determine if it's a good buy.

Pest-Control Products

In the past, pest-control products were primarily agricultural chemicals packaged for consumer use. Today the home gardener is reluctant to use such products because of their potential harm to humans and the environment. It is now more widely understood that broad-spectrum pesticides kill our good insects too, which destroys the balance of predator and prey that keeps insect populations under control naturally.

Fortunately, there are now many more natural nontoxic pesticides available both at garden centers and home improvement stores. The prices are comparable, but the natural products may take longer to do the job, so you must buy more. But again, it is worth the extra cost to protect the environment from excessive chemical use. And for gardeners, they are safer to apply, store, and dispose of over the long term.

Green Choices

Before you resort to a pest-control product, whether natural or chemical, try this first: many pests and problems can be solved by applying a strong jet of water to the foliage and branches of a tree, shrub, vine, or perennial. This not only cleans the leaves, it drives the pests away with water pressure. This has long been known as "syringing a plant." It can be done weekly as a preventative, which keeps pest numbers so low they rarely cause a problem. This is doubly beneficial for dusty plants, which are often attacked by spider mites that cling to the underside of a leaf, sucking out its juices in shady comfort. If you syringe your plants and let them dry before adding a natural pest-control product, it will be doubly effective.

There are many sources of home brews that can be used to create natural pesticides. These recipes call for ordinary materials, but here are a few tips to be sure your recipe turns out exactly right. Whenever a recipe calls for dish soap or ammonia, avoid any that contain special additives such as fragrances or sudsing agents. Those sold in health food stores or the less expensive types, such as house brands sold in a general supermarket, are the most reliable.

Ivory® dish soap is favored by golf course greenskeepers as a mild solution to wash oils off the grass. It's a good choice for cleaning houseplants and rinsing pollution off outdoor plants in the city. When using bleach, choose Clorox® or Pure because other, little-known brands may have altered formulas less suitable for plants. Test any homemade recipes on a small part of your plant to ensure they are compatible. Then wait forty-eight hours before applying the rest.

Your Own Pesticides, Fertilizers, and Weed Killers—Naturally!

Until the rise of the agricultural chemical industry, farmers and gardeners had to create their own formulas for killing insects and controlling weeds. These are often our best "green" choices too, since they're composed of ordinary household items.

Small-Budget Buy

If you live in the country or have a large homesite, you can get a better price on fertilizer and all sorts of other things at a farm or agricultural supply house. These places are geared to sell those items as agricultural products, which are exempt from sales taxes. At a retail consumer store you are not considered a farmer and therefore sales tax is charged. Not only will you save on tax, but these suppliers are geared to supply quantities of seed for cover crops, pastures, and erosion control mixes. If you are buying in bulk, shop where the farmers do; it can really add up to savings!

Homemade Pesticides

Insecticidal soap: Mix 4 tablespoons liquid dish soap into 1 gallon of water, then spray on plants. Kills aphids, spider mites, and many other insect pests.

Black fly control: Add 1 tablespoon plain ammonia to a quart of water and pour onto the soil.

White fly control: Spray leaves to control white flies with a combination of 2 tablespoons liquid dishwashing detergent and a gallon of water. You can also vacuum them up with a handheld vacuum cleaner held a few inches away from a plant's leaves.

Natural plant controls: Marigolds *(Tagetes erecta)* are planted in vegetable gardens because they repel some soilborne nematodes, which are microscopic worms that infect plant roots. Plant marigolds throughout a garden for more widespread protection.

Pepper spray: Combine long, red cayenne peppers or powder with water in a blender. You'll find both peppers and powdered peppers in the Mexican spice section of a supermarket for half the price of the traditional spices. They're said to control ants, spiders, cabbage worms, caterpillars, and tomato hornworms. Add pureed garlic or onion to control an even broader spectrum of pests.

Ant control: Try sprinkling ground, dried cayenne peppers into anthills to evict the entire nest. Sometimes cayenne pepper spray on plants will discourage deer from browsing, but only until it's washed off by sprinklers or rain.

Red spider mite control: These pests can be controlled with a spray of leftover coffee.

Homemade Fertilizer

A California Master Gardener has a special concoction she uses with great success. Whether or not it is less expensive than commercial products is difficult to tell, but it is nontoxic and completely safe for food crops. Combine in a gallon container:

¼ cup Epsom salts
¼ cup baking powder
¼ cup rubbing alcohol
¼ cup plain ammonia
1 8-ounce can of beer
6 aspirin

Add water to fill the container. Stir or shake to dissolve the aspirin. Spray leaves or drench soil around the plants.

Homemade Weed Killer

For weeds growing in paving cracks: Add a few tablespoons of salt to boiling water and pour it (still hot) over the weeds. To prevent new sprouts, sprinkle salt in the cracks. Beware of overdoing it as excess salt may dissolve with rainwater in runoff, harming other plants nearby.

Homemade Fungicide

For mildew, blackspot, or rust: Mix 3 teaspoons baking soda and 1 teaspoon liquid dish soap into 1 gallon of water and spray plants.

Other Cool Homemade Stuff

Deer Repellent: Mix 1 egg white in a blender container full of water and blend on low speed. Spray the mixture on plants. Repeat after rains or as needed.

Deer or Pet Repellent: Mix cayenne pepper powder with water in a blender. Spray on plants. This also works for animals (including puppies) that chew plants.

Fleabane: A 2-For-1 Plant

If you read through old books on medieval herbals, you'll inevitably find plant references to the problem of fleas, which ultimately spread the Black Plague through Europe. Before pesticides it was common to toss herbs over the floor of a home, pub, or castle to drive out pests that infested beds and rarely washed clothing. The oils in some garden herbs proved to be effective flea repellents, leading to the common name of "flea bane." The most famous and effective is *Mentha pulegium*, an easy-to-grow member of the mint family. For a budget household, you can select perennials for the garden, or you can choose a 2-for-1 plant that not only looks attractive but also adds to your ability to naturally control fleas in the home and, most of all, on your pets. Plant it in the yard where Fido hangs out and he'll absorb the oils into his coat. Or simply cut fresh branches and strip the leaves to line the bottom of a doghouse. Dry the herbs and leaves to stuff a mattress, which naturally discourages the pests through the winter months. Some of these herbs may also discourage ticks as well. See the facing page for some other easy-to-grow plants that have historically been grouped among the fleabanes.

Slugs: Pour some beer into a tin pie pan or other shallow container and place it in the garden. Slugs and snails can't resist the yeast, crawl in, and get trapped in the pan. You can intensify the attractiveness of this bait by adding a pinch of brewer's yeast. (Note: if they do not drown, you will still have to kill them.)

Climbing Pests: Those insects that must crawl up tree trunks to complete their lifecycles can be stopped by a sticky ring of molasses painted around the trunk a few feet from the bottom. The pests become bogged down in the molasses. Reapply when it dries out and loses its stickiness, or gets washed off by rain.

Common Name	Botanical Name	Comments
Fleawort	*Erigeron canadense*	annual
Wormwood	*Artemisia absinthum*	shrubby perennial
Tansy	*Tanacetum vulgare*	perennial

Some Tips on Pest Control Stuff That's Inexpensive or Free

Soft-bodied snails, slugs, and caterpillars have a difficult time crawling over sharp, granulated materials such as diatomaceous earth. This is a common, nontoxic, naturally occurring product used in swimming pool filters, so pool owners may already have it for that purpose. It is also deadly to ants and can be put down an ant hill for a control where kids, pets, and livestock are present. The diatomaceous earth causes the ants' exoskeletons to dehydrate enough to destroy the colony.

Another barrier to soft-bodied pests is sandpaper, which makes a useful barrier when it's cut into collars fitted around young plants. Recycle sanding disks, which are shaped into a convenient collars already, and which are typically discarded by cabinetmakers, auto body shops, and school wood shops.

2 Shop 'Til You Drop:
Get a bargain every time.

1-Gallon Perennials for Sun

Shopping is a woman thing. It's a contact sport like football. Women enjoy the scrimmage, the noisy crowds, the danger of being trampled to death, and the ecstasy of the purchase.

— Erma Bombeck

The simple act of acquiring plants is among the most satisfying shopping experiences. Installing these new candidates into the garden, particularly in spring, touches something primal in all of us that responds to this season when life returns from winter. Unlike many things we purchase at a store, plants are living, so the way we buy them takes a bit more care to get a healthy, vigorous individual at the lowest price possible.

Plants are second only to food in the amount of care they require while on retail display. Like lettuce, a wilted annual flower may never come back no matter how much moisture it gets later. And like bread, once the freshness has gone out of it, its value vanishes altogether. Day-old bread tastes nothing like fresh bread, and a plant too long in a retail setting will never become a vigorous, floriferous adult.

You must consider three things when shopping for plants. First is your budget, which limits how much you have to spend. Second is your level of horticultural knowledge, which dictates how well you can evaluate a plant. Third is the amount of time you have to devote to gardening or for a plant to mature.

Perhaps the most important factor when plant shopping is avoiding impulse buys. If you don't come prepared with a strong idea of what you need, you'll be vulnerable to buying plants that *are* truly fabulous, and possibly at a great price, too, but they may

Veni, vidi, VISA.
I came, I saw, I charged it.

not fit your climate or into your landscape design. If a plant really catches your eye, write down its name, then research it to find out if it will be successful in your garden.

What You Buy Dictates *Where* You Buy

While comparison shopping there are many details to absorb, from evaluating material quality to product workmanship, freshness, and style. In addition, knowing where you are likely to find what you want at the highest quality for the best price is the synthesis of all this data. Shopping is a many-faceted process that goes far beyond a simple act of "find it and buy it."

Our parents and grandparents bought everything they needed from a local nursery (if they didn't get it for free from a relative or neighbor!), which was later renamed "the garden center." In recent years many new kinds of stores and chains have cropped up that have changed the landscape of plant sales. Greater choices allow you to save a lot of money on plants *if* you know

where to get the best value for that particular kind of plant.

Plants are assembled into a few basic groups, about which a little knowledge will help you to understand where to buy them and why. Understanding the longevity and lifecycle of the plants you like helps you to make decisions in the marketplace that are right for your time and budget constraints.

Annuals

Examples of annuals include viola, zinnia, and marigold (as well as literally hundreds of others). While they may seem to be the least expenive kind of plant to buy, an annual is actually the *most*

Buying Seed Firsthand

Nothing is quite so beautiful as a display of beautiful seed packets. Each one of them is like a promise of color or food or whimsical plants we can grow for holidays. The ability to reach out and touch a packet, to feel that living seed inside is what has kept Ferry-Morse in garden centers, supermarkets, and home improvement stores for nearly 150 years. In-store seed sales allow you to buy everything you need all at once rather than splitting your purchases into mail order and local retail. More important, if you did buy seed by mail and forgot to order a particular plant, the Ferry-Morse type of display is the best way to pick it up in a timely fashion. Just be sure that you stick to the seeds on your list as these racks are the devil's playgrounds for impulse purchases!

expensive of all. This is because annuals (by their very definition) grow for just one year or growing season and then die. Its goal in life is to sprout from seed, mature, and then flower and set seed for the next year. When you buy annuals you need to select a vigorous individual capable of a fast start and immediate, prolific bloom. A poor doer might not catch up with the rest of the pack; tightly packed roots may never branch out into native soil—a poorly treated young annual may fail outright.

Annuals are started early in spring under lights in greenhouses so they're growing well by the time you're ready to buy them. But annuals are a one-shot deal in the garden. Oh, occasionally some might self-sow, but this is uncommon with today's hybrids. Typically, annuals are bought in six-packs or quart containers in quantities to create large bedding floral displays (though annuals can be vegetables and foliage plants, too).

Standard grow option: Purchase seeds.
Cheap grow option: Buy seedlings in six-packs.
Cheaper grow option: Buy seed and start your own.
***Free!* grow option:** Save the previous year's seed and grow them this year.

When you're shopping for bedding plants, pay close attention to the number of cells that are in the packs you buy. Those with eight cells obviously have more plants than more common six-cell containers, even though their prices can be similar.

Perennials

Examples of perennials include prairie coneflower, phlox, and lavender. A perennial is an herbaceous bedding plant that dies back to the ground in winter and sprouts again the next spring (usually—sometimes a perennial's growing season begins later in the year). Each year a perennial will grow more and produce new shoots that can be split off into entirely new plants in a process known as "division." They are long-lived flowering or foliage plants that take two to three years to reach marketable size. Some perennials require more or less time according to that species' growth habits. They

A quart container will be your "Best Buy" for established perennials.

Sometimes, small plant sellers like those you find at swap meets and street fairs sell their own backyard-grown stock. These can be some of your best buys for houseplants, succulents, and specialty plants.

will have to winter over in their containers, and growers usually have far more time and money invested in perennials. For this reason a perennial is often more expensive to buy. However, a perennial also lasts longer, so your investment is spread out over the lifespan of the plant, and you can also receive a bonus of free plants through division.

Standard grow option: Purchase one-gallon containers.

Cheap grow option: Buy quart-sized containers.

Cheaper grow option: Buy six-packs when available.

***Free!* grow option:** Trade divisions with friends.

Shrubs and Vines

Shrubs are woody plants that can range from small, groundhugging dwarf groundcovers to tree-sized monsters; all share the feature of woody branches. A shrub can live for a decade to a century, depending on the species. Shrubs require many years at a grower to reach saleable size. For this reason, shrubs will be far more expensive than bedding plants to buy, but due to their longevity they are much less expensive overall. With these plants it's even more important to remember that, no matter what size it is at purchase, they all mature to the same height and width of the particular species. Buying older, five-gallon container specimen shrubs is among the most expensive of all purchases since you are paying for instant gratification.

Standard grow option: Buy five-gallon containers.

Cheap grow option: Buy one-gallon containers.

Cheaper grow option: Buy balled-and-burlapped specimens.

Cheapest grow option: Buy bare-root shrubs or vines.

***Free!* grow option:** Salvage and transplant from a demolition site.

Trees

A California study conducted several years ago sought to put to rest once and for all the question whether paying more for a larger container tree is really worth the expense. Trees grown in five- and fifteen-gallon containers were compared to larger specimens grown in a two-foot-square wooden box; the larger specimens cost *hundreds* of dollars. The results showed the five-gallon specimens caught up to the fifteen-gallon ones in a year or two, which was expected. But the big surprise was that the fifteen-gallon tree overtook the boxed tree and exceeded its height in a relatively short time. Why? Because the root systems of the boxed trees were too compact to allow them to grow quickly once they were transplanted. This tells us that the optimal size of a container-grown tree is fifteen gallons, which provides good size and fast growth for a more moderate price. But trees are sold bare root as well, particularly fruit trees. Bare root is the least expensive way to buy trees because they are dug from the field while they're dormant and then sold during the right season in your area. And their roots spread out from the base unhindered by containers at any age, which makes them healthier and far more drought resistant.

> ## Small-Budget Buy
>
> Timing is everything when it comes to bargain shopping. Retail garden centers sell bare-root dormant roses during early spring in most areas. They often buy truckloads of them and heel (bury) the roots into damp sand or sawdust while they're on sale. Those roses that don't sell by the end of bare-root season are potted up and sold for a much higher price later on, when they're in leaf and flower. If you buy bare-root roses when they are in season, you can indeed purchase the very same rose for half the price.

Standard grow option: Purchase fifteen-gallon containers.

Cheap grow option: Purchase five-gallon containers.

Cheaper grow option: Buy bare-root trees.

***Free!* grow option:** Grow from seed or cutting.

Who Sells Plants Retail?

Every gardener wants to know where to find the best deal on plants. The answer depends on the kind of plant you seek. For that reason, this discussion of plant retailers will be relative to the previously listed plant types and the various growing options indicated for each.

There are two categories of retailer. One is a traditional garden center, which is the old-fashioned neighborhood nursery. The other is the chain store also known as a "big box" store. The vast majority of plants sold at retail are sold through one type or the other.

The Traditional Garden Center or GC

There is nothing more wonderful than finding an independent garden center stuffed with fabulous plants you don't see every day. These retail stores are managed by real plant lovers who stock ordinary plants augmented by a wide range of less-known specialties. Among these can be exotic food plants, natives, drought-resistant species for water conservation, unusual alpine succulents for colder climates, and strange herbs that only gour-

The traditional garden center is the place to find service, unusual plants, and quality trees and shrubs.

mets recognize. Shopping there is dangerous because these options make it really hard to stay within your budget.

The prices at independent stores are usually higher because they are buying from smaller specialty growers. They also can't get the quantity discounts that chains receive from larger growers. However, they are often the only place to find unusual perennials and shrubs as well as quality trees. These are the special plants that make your garden stand out as uniquely yours.

Independent garden centers are without question the best places to buy trees because the trees will be well cared for. In other retail situations where volume is key, trees suffer the most and are often potbound, broken, or poorly shaped. You want to purchase a top-quality sapling in which you can confidently invest *years* awaiting its maturation. Buying a tree at discount to save a few dollars just doesn't pay off in the long run. The chances of twisted roots, pests, and disease are serious consequences that can wipe out your investment.

One benefit of GCs is that they are smaller, privately owned stores. This gives the owner or manager more leeway to negotiate with you in order to make a large sale. Because a GC is the best place to place a special order for something unique, or to order a large quantity of bedding plants in a specific size and color, there is always an opportunity to negotiate for a better deal. Do not hesitate to ask for a quantity discount if you're spending big bucks. This goes for buying tons of bedding color or plants for a special event such as a wedding or party. Or maybe you're landscaping a new home and are buying a lot of plants at once.

Green Choices

Many neighborhood garden centers are very conscious of whom they buy from and how those companies use resources and treat the environment. They are the best source of truly organic seedlings for the vegetable garden because you can trust that they do indeed buy locally. They also tend organic plants in their inventory in such a way that does not contaminate them while

Tightwad Gardening Tip

Never assume that a plant on sale at a big box store is suited to your local climate. Buyers aren't always knowledgeable and may be placing orders for many stores at once. You are likely to find perennials, shrubs, and vines that are not winter hardy for your area. Similarly, cold-loving species can be sold at warm-climate stores. Know your hardiness zone and that of the plant on sale before making a purchase, because if it won't make it through the first winter or summer, it's no bargain at all.

Bargain Hunter's Quick Glance Retailer Guide

Below are the most common plant groups and the retail location where you can find a good bargain on a healthy plant.

GC Garden Center   **BB** Big Box

Specialty perennials: **GC**	Quantity bedding plants: **BB**	Large succulents: **GC**
Annuals: **BB**	Specimen trees: **GC**	Novelty succulents: **BB**
Cutting annual varieties: **GC**	Color vines: **BB**	Houseplants: **BB**
Specific colored annuals: **GC**	Herbs: **GC**	Fruit trees: **GC**
Ordinary seeds: **BB**	Organic seedlings: **GC**	Palms: **BB**
Unusual seed varieties: **GC**	Hedges: **BB**	Shade/accent Trees: **GC**
Ordinary perennials: **BB**	Groundcovers: **GC**	

they're on display. The garden center also promotes other green practices such as the use of water conservation plants and the planting of local natives that contribute to wildlife and the environment. For those who wish to make socially conscious investments in their plants and are willing to pay for it, support the independent store to keep them from being crowded out by the big box stores.

The Big Box

We all know the names of the two largest home improvement superstore chains that dominate the American marketplace. They are virtually identical in the minds of the consumer, and both maintain massive garden centers at their stores. These companies are able to take advantage of the quantity purchase, obtaining massive numbers of bedding plants at the lowest wholesale price possible. They sell at such a narrow margin that the mark-up can be minimal, making them the least expensive places to shop for plants, bar none.

The big box stores are a great place to pick up annuals and perennials, but only just after they arrive in the store because care can be unpredictable from store to store. Fortunately, these stores take deliveries every day and their stock cycles in and out quickly, keeping most of it fresh. Their staff may not be as dedicated as an independent GC, and plant stock can languish if there are extremes of heat or cold or unseasonable weather. This can be as simple as failure to close the shade cloth roof because nobody is paying attention, which can burn a whole table of stock in a matter of hours.

But, it is possible to find some really good perennials at a big box store. These one-gallon plants are well developed, blooming, and a great value. Many are even so overgrown they're ready to divide (two plants in one!). Just be aware some perennials may not be well labeled, containing little to no growing info. If you're not plant knowledgeable this can be really hit and miss.

With all annuals and perennials sold in six-packs or quarts, be careful to buy only fresh plants. Either special order them or know when deliveries are usually made and plan to shop soon afterward. At a big box store, you can get more plants for less money than just about anywhere else.

Another thing to bear in mind with a big box store concerns trees and shrubs. Sometimes you can find great deals

Today's Branded Plant

Some years ago the United States Patent Office started granting plant patents to hybridizers. This meant these folks would thus own all the progeny of a patented new variety and nobody could grow it without their permission. The idea was to license the plant to a wholesale grower, who would kick back a royalty to the patent holder for each one they grow and sell. Flower Carpet Groundcover Roses, which are promoted by an extensive public relations campaign, are among the most famous patented plants. Now everyone is trying to patent their new varieties and the market is full of them. Are they better? Not necessarily. Do they cost more? Sure. The grower passes the extra cost on to you. With many you can find a nearly identical variety for less because it's not encumbered by the additional costs of the patent system.

This tickseed is a private brand as shown by the unusual container designed to make it stand out against similar, or perhaps even identical, varieties in generic containers.

There's no reason why fruit trees can't also serve as landscape trees because they offer just as much spring and fall color as fruitless forms.

on trees and shrubs because these sell at rock-bottom prices. Many stores are really good at ordering locally suitable plants, and the earlier in the season you shop, the better your choice. However, plants that have been on display a long time, by mid- or late season, may have suffered; inspect each potential purchase carefully. Most big box stores carry only the most basic trees and shrubs, and even these can be hit and miss. You really must shop there knowing you may not find the plant you want

because their stock of woodies is unreliable. Plus, the larger
containers of trees and shrubs are more difficult to water and
they are often left to dry out one too many times. Because they
don't grow fast like bedding plants you may find individuals
that have been there far too long and have developed overly
dense or distorted roots. Sometimes a poor root system will
never regain a healthy shape and cannot be expected to grow
vigorously, ever.

One thing about a big box store that most knowledgeable
gardeners have discovered is that you *can* find great surprises
there. Some plants may be priced that are the result of pric-
ing errors, remnants from the grower, or just a corporate snafu.
While shopping for a Japanese maple for a TV makeover show
we found an incredible specimen at a New Jersey Home Depot
for one-third of the price you'd find at a GC. Here in California I
found an expensive, slow-growing succulent tree sold at similar
discount. They can be unusually large or rare specimens and sell
for an amazingly low price. So keep your eyes peeled for these
bargains because they can be the best in town.

Caveat Emptor – Inspect Before You Buy

When you buy a plant, you have the right to a top-quality specimen every time. But in a typical plant display you'll find some
individuals are in better shape than others. A quality plant will
be topnotch in three areas: roots, shape, and health. Use these
handy inspection tips as an aid in evaluating every plant you buy,
particularly the larger and more expensive trees and shrubs.

Roots

When buying plants in containers avoid those whose roots
appear on the surface, are growing out the drain holes, or are
matted together. For balled-and-burlapped stock avoid a dry,
loose rootball. For bare-root stock avoid dry, damaged, crushed,
and broken roots.

Trunks

Strive for perfect, undamaged bark. Inspect the trunk for gouges,
scars, tears from lost branches, and nicks around the bottom.
A trunk should be upright, straight, and evenly balanced, not
slanted or twisted.

Branching

Select a specimen for perfect size and proportion. Avoid a shrub with open spots in its branching structure, broken branches, oversized branches that don't conform to its natural shape, or a lopsided form. Shrubs lacking lower branches or those that are poorly shaped at the base will never repair themselves.

Foliage

Select plants with lush, perfectly colored leaves. Avoid any with discolored leaves, unusual leaf drop, wilted leaves, or curled leaves, which are all signs of pests and disease. Beware if a plant is shedding leaves out of season or if its leaves are abnormally small.

Bedding Plants

Buy young, vigorous seedlings. Slide out a plant to inspect its rootball, which tells you how old it is. Choose those with the largest abundance of soil and avoid any with dense rooting. Avoid plants with spindly stems and elongated growth from lack of light. Poor shape or irregular growth habit rarely corrects itself.

Pests

Avoid plants that shed little white flies when you shake them, or those with unusual granular materials coming out of the drainage holes. Inspect the undersides of leaves for tiny spots or webby material.

Dos and Don'ts of Plant Buying

- Never assume that just because a plant is for sale locally it is suited to your climate.
- Don't believe everything you read on a plant tag; one size does *not* fit all climates.
- Shy away from "miracle" problem-solving plants; they just have a catchy sales pitch.
- Don't assume the salesperson really knows what he or she is talking about.
- Always know the sun exposures in your garden before you buy a plant for a particular spot.
- Always select the very best plant in the display.
- If you can't plant right away, store new plants in a sheltered, moist location.

Living Christmas Trees

Every year millions of evergreen trees are cut for the holidays and Americans spend an incredible amount of money for something they use for just a few weeks. Then those millions of trees must be disposed of, which is a nightmare for urban waste management departments. The whole concept of a cut tree is terribly costly in so many ways. It makes sense to rethink having a cut Christmas tree and explore a living alternative.

Living trees can be planted into the landscape after the holidays to become a beautiful part of the garden. The first year it will be grown indoors in its container, then planted out in the garden when spring arrives. When designing landscapes for my clients, I always ask if they would like a pine, fir, or spruce in the front yard to decorate for the holidays. We plant this special tree relative to a window for best enjoyment from indoors. In colder climates real snow on a decorated outdoor tree is always more beautiful than artificial flocking on an indoor tree. And, although an indoor tree is the traditional way to celebrate the holidays, an outdoor tree decorated with weatherproof lights and ornaments can be just as satisfying. It is the green alternative to dead holiday tree consumption that teaches a powerful ecological message to new generations.

A successful living Christmas tree must be a species that is well adapted to the local climate. Many of the most beautiful and symmetrical conifers cannot thrive where the winters are very warm and may gradually decline no matter how much special care you provide. If you're in doubt, discuss this with a local garden center expert because he or she will carry conifers suitable for your climate.

The species you choose must also be sized so it can easily be decorated without exceeding the height of your free-standing ladder. Conifers can be deceivingly small when they are young, but then mature to monstrous proportions, so it's vital you select a variety that is sized for your yard and this purpose. City and many suburban homes will find fertile ground among dwarf forms of otherwise large forest trees of America, Europe, and Asia.

Above all, a good living Christmas tree should maintain a naturally conical shape throughout its life span. Some Christmas trees such as Scotch pine are commercially sheared into a more perfect conical shape and are sold as juveniles. This species can reach from twenty-five to fifty feet tall at maturity, which would be far too large for most yards. Scotch pine, as with all forms of topiary, may require you shear them once or twice a year to maintain their smaller size and geometric shape.

The best outdoor Christmas trees are smaller conifers that remain small enough to decorate even when they mature.

Conifers that bear attractive foliage and coloring offer both an outdoor holiday tree and cuttings to trim off for indoor décor.

- Know the size of any tree or shrub at maturity before you buy it.
- If the plant dies soon after planting, take it back to the garden center for a refund.
- Plants intended as gifts rarely grow well in the garden so avoid buying these as landscape plants.
- Never remove stakes or supports until after a plant is securely in the ground.

Double Duty Plants

Value is a word that television shopping channels have put front and center. It refers to just how much a product offers relative to its price. A high-value product will be one that really works hard for very little cost, and these are among the most prolific sellers. This concept applies to plants in your garden, as well. Most plants give you one primary value, which is beauty, or something more practical such as shade. Other plants give you a harvest of food or fragrance, and even supplies for natural décor and crafts. These are items you'd otherwise have to buy at a store. So when you find a plant that gives you aesthetic beauty *and* problem solving *plus* a secondary harvest of food, décor, or craft supplies, it literally doubles the overall value of the plant. Essentially you get two plants for the price of one! That 2-for-1 plant is indeed a real bargain.

Today everyone is waking up to the value of growing their own fruit. With a global food supply, there is no other way to ensure your fruit is free of chemicals or human handling diseases such as salmonella. A bonus of homegrown fruit is the possibility of having a crop large enough to freeze, dry, or can for the months ahead.

Fruit trees are among our best 2-for-1 plants because they live for decades and produce fruit every year (unless a freeze interrupts their blooming cycle). Unlike vegetable crops, you only need to plant a fruit tree once. Plus, you get lots of ornamental value when a stone fruit tree bursts into vivid spring bloom; it rivals the showiest ornamentals. The idea that a fruit tree must be in an orchard or grow separate from an ornamental garden is wrong. Fruit trees belong in our front or backyards and will become the most prolific returns of all your home improvement investments.

Common 2-for-1 Fruit Trees

Some common ornamentals can be substituted by fruiting plants that offer the same beauty and color *plus* provide a bonus of edible fruit.

Botanical Name	Ornamental Variety	Fruiting Variety
Buxus sempervirens	Boxwood	Blueberry
Chaenomeles japonica 'Texas Red'	Flowering Quince	Quince
Malus hybrid	Crabapple	Apple
Parthenocissus quinquefolia	Virginia Creeper	Eastern table grapes
Prunus serrulata 'Kwanzan'	Ornamental Cherry	Fruiting cherry
Pyrus calleryana 'Bradford'	Bradford Pear	Fruiting pear
Rosa	Hybrid Tea	*Rosa rugosa*

Throughout this book you'll see special examples of other 2-for-1 plants when they apply to the various chapters. These are wonderful choices that can turn your home landscape into a treasure trove of beautiful cut material, supplies, foods, medicine, seasonings, fragrances, and decorative items. Unlike seasonal flowers that are here today and gone next year, the 2-for-1 plant is more long-lived and becomes a permanent component in your garden.

Some of the Best 2-for-1 Plants

Name	Landscape value	Secondary value
Corkscrew willow	Shade tree	Twisted branches for cutting
Pomegranate	Flowering accent tree	Fruit that also dries to use for décor
Grape vines	Arbor cover for shade	Fruit, leaves for Greek food
Blueberry	Hedge	Fruit
Conifer	Evergreen tree	Outdoor holiday décor
Pyracantha	Hedge	Bright orange berries for the holidays
Lavender	Color and drought resistance	Dried flowers, scented crafts
Rugosa rose	Hedge or single accent	Famous for its medicinal fruit

Not-So-Big Outdoor Christmas Tree Candidates

This carefully compiled list features well tested varieties of otherwise large forest trees. These dwarf forms should not require pruning except for an occasional shaping. Choosing a dwarf variety means the Christmas tree retains its perfect shape and beauty for decades to come without increasing your burden of landscape maintenance.

Botanical Name	USDA Zone	Height (ft.)	Width (ft.)
Chamaecyparis obtusa 'Gracilis'	4–8	10	5
Cupressus arizonica 'Blue Pyramid'	6–9	20	10
Cupressus virginiana 'Cupressifolia'	4–9	15	6
Juniperus scopulorum 'Cologreen'	3–7	20	6
Picea glauca 'Conica'	2–8	8	4
Picea glauca 'Densata'	2–8	25	12
Picea pungens glauca 'Fat Albert'	2–8	15	10
Thuja occidentalis 'Emerald'	4–8	15	4

3 Free Dirt:
Feed your soil on the cheap.

A rind is a terrible thing to waste. Compost.

— Bumper sticker

The foundation of all gardening is soil. Unfortunately, no homesite has perfect dirt, so there is always a need to improve soil conditions to make them better for plants. The things we add to soils are varied both in their role and cost. Some are voluminous while others come in a small box. But what all share is the ability to create a better environment for a plant to live. And, of course, we want to do this for as little cash as possible. Fortunately, nature makes this easy, if you know how to obtain and use economical alternatives to expensive products.

Most things added to the soil fall into one of three categories, each serving a completely different purpose.

Fertilizer: This is a material or product that adds nutrients to the soil to increase its fertility. There are slow-acting organic fertilizers such as cow manure, and there are synthetic "rocket fuel" fertilizers such as Miracle Gro®. Fertilizers may be sold both in liquid or dry forms, packaged or in bulk.

Soil Amendment: Amendments are tilled into the soil to change its texture or structure. An amendment is usually a form of organic matter, which may be coarse like shavings or fine in texture like compost. Adding amendments can help a soil drain better or help it hold moisture. Some can even improve fertility. Amendments are sold in bags or in bulk.

Mulch: This is any material laid upon the ground around a plant to cover the

The best new garden center products are organic fertilizers created in such a way that makes them as easy to apply as synthetic fertilizers (below).

This light, sandy loam soil is every gardener's dream because it's well drained, fertile, and easy to work.

There is no perfect soil, and no matter what type you have in your backyard, it will benefit from annual additions both of amendments and fertilizers to maintain consistent fertility.

soil to block weeds or retain moisture. Most of the time a mulch is an organic material such as ground bark, but wood chips and even gravel are used as well. Mulch may be sold in bulk to give an entire garden a uniform look, or in bags for smaller spot applications.

Green Choices

If you are using synthetic fertilizers, you must reapply them often to keep the soil fertile. That's why they can become expensive. When you grow plants organically, the additives you'll use don't work as quickly, but they maintain their effectiveness on plant health far longer. Compare this difference to being tired. You can eat a candy bar to pep yourself up, but it won't last and you'll crash with a blood sugar drop. The alternative is to eat a healthy, natural meal that won't give you that instant pep, but it will sustain you more evenly over many hours.

An Organic Approach

Almost everything discussed in this chapter will be considered organic materials. They are suitable for an organic food garden or a "greener" ornamental one. This is a mix-and-match world that includes a huge array of things you may never have thought to add to your garden. The most economical choices will be those that are available close to your yard since haul-

ing material is a big cost (and time) factor. For example, if you live in a rice-growing region, rice hulls are inexpensive and plentiful. The same is true for equestrian communities and horse manure.

Green Choices

We don't live in a perfect world, but there's huge pressure to become a "perfect" organic gardener. We try hard to follow all the rules, but the reality is that budget and time constraints limit our choices. Gardening itself is important no matter how you do it, and successful yields is the real goal, not necessarily the process. So if you have to break a few rules now and then, don't feel you've committed a mortal sin. Keep the perfect organic gardening model as your ideal and strive to follow it knowing that nothing is perfect and neither are gardeners.

What makes traditional gardening different from the organic approach is the use of synthetic fertilizers. These are rated by the three numbers on the label, which indicate the percentages of nitrogen, phosphorus, and potassium (NPK) in the formula. For example, a common granular all-purpose product is 16-16-16. Compare that to cow manure, which is about 2-5-2.

Rich mixtures of compost and other organic matter are exceptional materials to amend poor or heavy soils, helping them to drain better and resist compaction.

Some potting soil contains slow-release fertilizer integrated into the mix so your veggies or flowers benefit from nutrients available deep within their root zone from day one.

The numbers don't tell the whole story, though. When you look at the organic materials in the charts that follow, remember that they do more than just add nutrients, they contain all sorts of smaller minerals, microorganisms, and soil conditioning abilities.

These charts are prepared to illustrate the vast potency differences so the new organic gardener discovers where the nutrients lie. It also helps if you compare your sources and their potency for the best value per dollar you spend. Fortunately, many are free, which is one of the beautiful things about organic gardening.

Top Three Synthetic Garden Fertilizers and Their NPK Analysis

Miracle Gro® 24-8-16
Spectrum 15-30-15
Shultz 10-5-10

Manure Content Comparison

These manures are better fertilizers, and due to the amount of undigested fiber in some of them, they also make fine soil conditioners.

Type	Nitrogen	Phosphorus	Potassium
Bat guano	13	5	2
Poultry manure	4.0	3.2	1.9
Goat manure	2.77	1.78	2.88
Cow manure	2.0	0.54	1.92
Rabbit manure	2.0	1.33	1.20
Sheep manure	2.0	1.0	2.5
Hog manure	1.0	0.75	0.85
Horse manure	0.7	0.34	0.52

Sometimes you'll find manures mixed into bulk materials such as straw or shavings. This is often termed "bedding" and can include manure from a number of animals. Note how low the content numbers are for the bulk materials list compared to that of the manures. Bedding itself can drag down an overall fertility rating. When evaluating bedding, note the amount of actual manure present. If the bedding is composed of shavings, which contain no nitrogen, and it is combined with a little horse manure that is only 0.7 percent nitrogen, you're getting no boost whatsoever. In fact, due to a complex process by which soil breaks down woody matter, your soil can actually end up *less* fertile than when you started. This is why knowing the nutrient content really matters.

Bulk Materials

These materials make better mulches or soil amendments and may benefit from being used with a supplemental nitrogen source.

Type	Nitrogen	Phosphorus	Potassium
Shredded corn-stalks	2.5	0.07	0.04
Bean straw	1.2	0.25	1.25
Alfalfa hay	1.5	0.3	1.5
Wheat straw	0.6	0.20	1.1
Seaweed	0.2	0.1	0.6
Leaf litter	0.13	0.08	0.03
Wood shavings	-	0.02	0.01

Anyone can go out and buy manures or compost by the bag from a home improvement store, but using them to treat a sizable area becomes expensive. For many types of organic matter such as manures, obtaining it in bulk is the most economical way to amend a sizeable garden.

To amend raised beds, try using buckets, such as the ones cat litter comes in, to transport materials. Another method is to use heavy-duty plastic garbage bags. Fill them only one-third full or less to prevent tearing, then pack them into the trunk of your car or haul them. If you don't own a pickup truck or can't find one to borrow, try renting a little trailer to haul behind your car. Beware of hauling right after it's rained because these materials, if they have been stored outdoors, can become considerably heavier to load and haul. This is why many experienced gardeners haul their soil materials in the dry, fall months to stockpile until they are ready to till it in spring.

The Manure Safari

In urban and high-density suburban communities, the most common large animal is the horse, often concentrated at boarding stables where manure is always plentiful. This is the best place to get started on your manure safari.

In some cases, the only way to buy manure is by the bag, so start keeping your eyes open for sales where the prices on cow manure may drop for a short time. That's the best time to stock up whether you need it right away or not. Bagged poultry manure, along with some other animal waste, rarely contains bedding materials. It may be composted and sterilized, which means it is free of weed seeds and not likely to "burn" plants. But again, this costs money.

The concept of a manure safari is to scope out inexpensive or free sources of bulk manures in your area. Remember that, to most people, manure is waste product that they must get rid of, and they are usually thankful that you are willing to pick it

Cattle produce the most weed-free manure, and there can be a great deal of it at dairies and stockyards where it is concentrated and easy to pick up.

up. This stuff won't be composted or sterilized, but that's never stopped old-fashioned gardeners from growing massive crops.

Dairies and Stockyards: Dairies and stockyards offer the best source of manure with minimal weed seeds. Cows have three stomachs, which means they digest more weed seeds than other livestock. (They do not digest all, however.) A dairy or stockyard is the best place to obtain large quantities that can turn a backyard kitchen garden into a really fabulous producer in a single season.

Farms: Farms are often rich in all sorts of manures. You may be able to clean out a chicken coop in exchange for some buckets of free, high-powered organic "fuel." Poultry manure has the richest amount of nitrogen of all livestock manures, and a small amount goes a long way.

Ranches: The environmental impact of manure runoff makes it mandatory for ranchers to strictly control accumulations, so you may be doing them a favor by carting it away.

Horse Stables: The equestrian set loathes flies, which are drawn to manures, and will do nearly anything to keep the shavings and manure off the property. You'll often find police stables in the midst of a city, and don't overlook racetracks where huge stables are located behind the scenes.

Fairs: Every year livestock are brought to state and local fairs, generating a great deal of concentrated manure.

Colleges and Universities: Those with agricultural or veterinary programs are excellent resources for manures and other byproducts.

Rooftop Pigeon Coops: City pigeon keepers keep the cages on the roofs of apartment buildings. While pigeon manure may be too potent to use directly, it can be mixed into rooftop vegetable garden soils or compost bins for a big fertility boost.

More Manure Sources: Pet stores (but only if it is not from cats or dogs), exotic bird breeders, petting zoos, wild animal parks.

Tightwad Gardening Tip

The best way to find people with large animals or those who raise livestock is through your local feed store (farmers' co-op). For those who breed anything from rabbits to goats, sheep, llamas, and miniature donkeys, this is ground zero where they all meet to buy feed and share news. A note on the feed store bulletin board about your needs may help you make some contacts.

Agricultural Byproducts

Many agricultural products must undergo extensive processing in order to become market-ready, and often there are organic byproducts that result. Some of these byproducts are in high demand such as cottonseed meal or olive pomace, which are turned over to other manufacturers. Among these processors are quality organic fertilizer makers who combine them in exact recipes for easy-to-use pellets. But pelleted organic fertilizers are expensive, if you can even find them locally. You'll save money and enjoy a great organic garden if you research what's available in your immediate area and whether it would make good compost or if it can be tilled straight into the soil. You'll derive benefits similar to the pellets for a fraction of the price.

Hulls and Shells

Grains such as rice, buckwheat, and oats are encased in thin, fibrous hulls. After harvest the grains are processed and the hulls removed. Rice hulls are one of the great, undiscovered soil amendments because they resist decomposition, are lightweight, and are finely textured. Although rice is only grown in certain areas, they will be an inexpensive or free resource if they're nearby. Contact your nearest state agricultural office to inquire whether there are any processing plants or farmers, co-operatives nearby. Often the hulls are stockpiled there and free if you pick them up.

Nuts also form within a hull, but these tend to be thick and fleshy. Inside a hard, dry shell holds the edible kernel within. The hulls are valuable because they will decompose (with time) and are excellent organic matter to hold open heavy soils such as adobe clay. Nut shells may also take a very long time to decompose, which makes them excellent as functional and decorative surface mulches depending on the type of nut. Ground walnut shells are in high demand for landscaping because of their den-sity, uniformity, and color. Walnut *hulls*, on the other hand, are not useful; they're too rich in tannin and can cause staining. Pecan shells are widely available in Southern states while almonds are a significant crop in California. Pea-nut shells are soft and fibrous, which makes them an excellent mulch or soil amendment. Packing houses that process fruits like peaches or cherries leave an abundance of pits, which may be of considerable value for soil improvement when they're crushed.

> ## Tightwad Gardening Tip
>
> Don't underestimate the beauty of ground walnut or pecan shells for pathway surfaces. Unlike gravel, these organic materials can mingle with the natural soil without contaminating it. For regions where traditional forest products aren't handy, the use of such unusual materials such as this is a beautiful and organic choice.

Pomace

Pomace is a term given to the residue of olives, fruits, and grapes after processing, either at packing houses or wineries. Pomace consists of skins and seed fragments that contain only scant quanti-ties of nutrients, but the seed makes a good soil amendment or addition to compost. Pomace is not as "clean" as hulls or shells, but it is usually free. It's far easier to handle if the pomace has had time to fully air dry before you transport it. This makes it more light-weight to move and less prone to fermentation odors, particularly

Straw is one of the most used mulches because a tightly packed bale can fit into most SUVs or mini-vans or even in the trunk of a large passenger car.

in the heat of summer. Grape pomace is a good product available in California and in all other American wine-producing regions.

Cotton Gin Waste

Cotton gin waste is another old-time byproduct of the Cotton Belt. Like hulls, cotton gin waste contains very little nutrition, but if obtained inexpensively enough it is useful for soil conditioning or for adding to a compost heap.

Straw

Straw is inexpensive, easy to buy, and nicely packed into an easy-to-handle bale. A bale will slide into the back of a minivan or the trunk of a larger passenger car. You can buy straw from feed stores and garden centers. Its origin is most often wheat, but you can also get rice straw and other forms unique to certain agricultural areas.

Straw is popular with vegetable gardeners as a surface mulch to block weeds between widely spaced rows and to keep your feet out of wet ground. It's easy to transport in a wheelbarrow, and a well-compressed bale opens up to a very large mass of material. Straw is used around the bases of the plants to keep them more evenly damp during very hot weather; it also shades the root zones and keeps them cool. After straw has decomposed over a growing season, it can be tilled back into the soil in the late fall or early spring.

For new homes and freshly graded homesites, erosion control is vital to keeping runoff from carrying away exposed soil particles. Straw is the least expensive material to do that. It also is often used by highway departments to broadcast over a new slope; then it's punched in with shovels to hold it in place over the rainy season. These anchorages make a perfect place for grass seed tossed for erosion control to lodge and grow. Anyone planting open spaces, slopes, and pastures on sloping ground will benefit from this technique.

Since straw is so easy to get, you can stockpile any excess in a corner of the garden to gradually break down. Or, open a whole bale and separate the flakes. Throw a few shovels of native soil in between each flake of straw as it piles up. This is a great way to begin a lazy gardener's compost pile. Occasionally add handfuls of fertilizer or manure with high nitrogen content to the pile along with anything else, such as old potting soil or kitchen refuse, to introduce microorganisms. Forget it for a year or two. The result will be an excellent amendment for clay soil that will go a long way for pennies.

Cover Crops and Green Manures

In the past, farmers didn't have the ability to haul truckloads of manure, and synthetic fertilizers weren't available, so they learned to grow their soil fertility. For centuries farmers planted fallow fields in temporary cover crops of leguminous plants. Legumes have the unique ability to transform nitrogen from the air and transfer it into the soil where they are growing, thus leaving the ground more fertile than before. These unique plants include many different types of clover, alfalfa, and peas. After a legume plant dies, there is a lot of nitrogen trapped in its stems and roots. When legumes are tilled into the earth, they release a boost of natural nitrogen.

Budget gardeners can take full advantage of this to improve larger sites and vegetable plots. Green manure is also the best

> ## Tightwad Gardening Tip
> Wheat straw bales occasionally contain grain heads with a few seeds attached. When planted, or if they volunteer from your straw mulch, let them grow into full-fledged wheat. These make beautiful, free craft materials for autumn decorating and flower arrangements.

Straw Bale Planters

If you have very poor soil and want raised beds right now, consider creating straw bale planters. You can actually do this on concrete too! Simply buy a bunch of bales and put them end-to-end to create an open rectangle. Fill the interior with native soil or potting soil to a depth of at least eighteen inches and plant away.

Place a single bale large-side down in a location that is too poorly drained to support a crop, or on concrete. Water the still-bound bale frequently and pile some manure or topsoil on top of it. A few chops with a shovel or stabs with a spading fork help the soil work into the center of the bale. Water some more. When the straw decomposes enough, the center of the bale will heat up. Plant squash or bean seeds in the loose material on top and they will germinate easily from the bottom heat. As they grow, they'll send their roots into the center of the bale, gradually loosening the bale deeper down. Wait until the second season and plant root crops right into this stuff that formerly supported the beans and squash. Depending on your climate you may be able to "farm" that straw bale for three years, or until it has disintegrated too much to hold plants. When the time comes to "bail" out of the project, cut the baling twine and use the now highly fertile organic matter in the rest of your garden.

Peaceful Valley Farm Supply

One of the most complete resources for organic gardening and soil care is Peaceful Valley Farm Supply in Northern California. http://www.groworganic.com

This online and paper catalog company evolved to serve gardeners growing for organic farmers' markets. But this source is also a favorite of gardeners in the city and suburbs, no matter what they grow or how much.

You can buy some cover crop seed that has been rhizocoated, which is an important benefit for legume seed. There is a beneficial organism that lives inside a legume's roots that is vital to its ability to process atmospheric nitrogen. Ordinarily a legume must accumulate the organisms from sparse populations already in the soil. But, seed that's rhizocoated is already wrapped in dormant, dry organisms waiting for moisture to "wake them up." Such concentrated populations allow a seedling to process nitrogen earlier in its life, thereby delivering more nitrogen into the soil when it's tilled under.

For seed that is not rhizocoated, you can buy inoculants formulated for a particular cover crop. The inoculant material is mixed with the seed prior to sowing, but it achieves the same results as the coated form. Inoculants not only benefit cover crops, they are equally useful in increasing yields from leguminous veggies such as peas and beans.

Peaceful Valley offers a full range of cover crop seed. They also sell mixtures tailored to offer cover crops with more visual diversity. The company also guarantees that if one kind of plant in the mix doesn't do well, there will be others to take its place. Their best-selling Soil Builder Mix runs about $1.50 per pound with an application range of 3 to 5 pounds per 1000 square feet. It contains five different types of soil-enhancing cover crop species that are ideal for small homesite applications, erosion control, and wildlife habitat. The seed is "raw" so you must purchase an inoculant for vetch or a combination product.

way to rehabilitate a homesite that has extensive grading and soil disturbance. Often when a house is built on subsoil, you must build the ground up considerably in order to have a successful garden.

Choosing the right legume for your region may require some professional guidance from a farm advisor or neighbor familiar with local conditions. Some legumes are sown in fall to prepare for a spring garden. You can do this every year if you wish, which will cause the soil to gradually grow richer and richer. Legume seeds are sold by organic garden outlets or local farm supply stores where they'll know the varieties and planting times that are best for your climate.

Budget Gardener's Secret Weapon

Planting cover crops isn't always possible for a variety of reasons, but here's a shortcut that achieves much the same result in the garden for only slightly more money. Alfalfa, a legume, is a common baled livestock feed, and when used to enhance soil, its nutrient content is nearly identical to that of some manures. Baled alfalfa is a compressed, preserved cover crop that you can take apart and spread throughout your garden. It can be used in lieu of straw as a mulch in the first year, then tilled in at season's end. If you spread it in fall, run your lawn mower over the alfalfa to further chop it into smaller bits that will be easier to work into the soil in spring. Or, just spread and till it in during fall to generate nutrients and add organic matter as it decomposes over winter. This technique is a budget gardener's secret weapon to starting a new garden on the road toward high fertility for very little cost compared to bagged compost and other similar products. Using a bale also adds ease of transportation to its features.

Hairy vetch, with its beautiful flowers, is a green manure legume that can deliver, or "fix," 60 to 120 pounds of nitrogen per acre when sown in recommended densities. This is just one of the many legumes grown to be tilled into soil to add both nitrogen and organic matter.

If you take the alfalfa idea a step further, consider yet another technique for green manure that costs a bit more—pelleted alfalfa feeds. Organic gardeners rave about these as ornamental mulches because they are an attractive and easy-to-use form of green manure. Pellets are simply alfalfa that's been chopped up and compressed into a more manageable form that can be used on food and herb gardens as well as for ornamental plants such as roses. Distribute the pellets into the soil or around a plant and in a short time they'll disintegrate into the ground, offering both nitrogen and organic matter.

Green Choices

Alfalfa pellets are a great alternative for urban gardeners who may not have access to much organic matter or manure. Although processing and packaging drives the price of pellets up, there is no better way to get a good start on organic gardening.

Confessions of a Dysfunctional Composter

I hate to admit it but I am a compost failure. In all my years of gardening I have never once created and maintained a functional compost pile. Perhaps it was due to the dry climate where I live or the fact that I just didn't have enough stuff to feed it. More often than not I put what I could compost directly into my awful clay-and-rocks soil to keep it from cementing back together again. During those years of "failure" it was not a total loss because that heap consumed tons of leaves and rotten fruit and garden refuse. And maybe I'd get a few shovels full of the good stuff now and then. Its value was that I had some place to put all that excess organic matter from garden and kitchen to avoid placing an added burden on the landfill. So if you aren't successful at composting, or if your yields, like mine, are too small to seemingly make much difference, just keep on gardening and composting. It all works out in the end.

Forest Byproducts

With high prices and slowdowns in the logging industry, the cost of forest byproducts has become limited and expensive. The landscape industry uses ground bark of various conifers as decorative mulch because of its beauty, uniform color, and texture. But this is so costly that landscapers use a very thin layer useful only for aesthetics. It's too thin a layer to obtain the other important benefits of mulching.

It takes a layer at least two inches thick to block weed germination, retain soil moisture, and shade the root zone as well as cover unattractive ground. The better choice is wood chips, the byproducts of many tree-and vegetation-related industries. The most common source is wood chips generated by tree trimming companies that chip their branches to reduce the cost of disposal. If there is a tree trimmer in the neighborhood running a chipping machine, don't hesitate to ask if you can have the chips. Be willing to offer them a six-pack or some money for the favor and be prepared to receive a large pile in the driveway.

Landfill composting programs are one of the smartest innovations in green urban waste management. They grind up the matter into chipped mulches, which are then made available for people in the community who are willing to load and haul it themselves.

Shavings are finer than wood chips and make a useful soil amendment, particularly where soils are heavy clay. The landscape industry uses nitrolized shavings, which are treated with an extra dose of synthetic nitrogen so that they can decompose without nitrogen losses in the soil. You can buy ordinary shavings in tightly packed bales, but this is not particularly cost effective. Strive for free sources such as a high school woodshop, the super source for urban gardeners scrounging for organic matter. The same is true for cabinetmakers' shops and lumberyards that cut wood to order for their customers. Don't overlook woodlots where firewood is sold, too, because there you'll find all sorts of bark and wood byproduct accumulations.

Cheap or Free Soil Solutions

These are some old-time solutions for pest control and nutrient deficiencies dating back to the times before the advent of agricultural chemicals.

Iron: If your plants become chlorotic (their leaves turn yellow while the veins remain green), they may be suffering from iron deficiency. Old-time farmers used to gather scrap iron such as wire or anything else that rusts, then throw them into a bucket of water. Keep refilling after water evaporates until you have a potent brew of "rust tea."

Fish: Wherever a plentiful supply of fish was available, early Native Americans would plant the remnants of freshly caught fish beneath corn plants. Fishermen, recycle your cleaned fish and cooks, reuse those fins and heads by planting them at least eight inches deep in the garden. This is considered the minimum to keep critters and odors at bay. Then allow a full year of decomposition before planting on top of this newly enriched soil.

Eggshells: One old New England practice was to plant a fresh egg under each tomato plant. It's easier to just collect your eggshells and do the same. The shells contain generous amounts of calcium and other nutrients that make your garden grow.

Sulfur: Sulfur deficiency in the soil can cause new leaves to turn yellow. A simple remedy uses a few match heads worked into the soil around the plant. If color returns to the leaves afterward, you have proved your soil lacks this micronutrient.

> ## Tightwad Gardening Tip
> Keep your eye on the weather. If your area has experienced flooding or heavy rains over a sustained period, many stables end up discarding a great deal of damaged alfalfa products, both baled and pelleted. Since water is the greatest threat to alfalfa as livestock feed, even the slightest moisture damage means it must be discarded. You may find they've set aside the spoiled bales or overly damp pellet bags from months before; they would be glad to get them off the property before a wayward animal decides to start munching on them. The same idea applies to feed stores, farms, and ranches.

Small, cheaply made compost and leaf mold bins should be in every gardener's backyard.

Compost and Leaf Mold

So much of what goes down your garbage disposal or into the garbage can be recycled into compost. Not only does composting relieve pressure on the landfills, it's good for the environment by returning natural materials back to the earth.

Compost is decomposed organic matter that is high in nutrients and makes an excellent soil conditioner. But it takes a tremendous amount of compost to support a garden of any size, so it's not uncommon to have to buy some as well.

Making A Compost Bin

These days there are a lot of different products out there to help you make compost quicker. These can simplify the process, but the cost rises for such a specialized product and they are limited in the amount of material they can handle at one time. For the frugal gardener with some space to devote to the process, larger, permanent bins are definitely the way to go.

By far the least expensive and oldest method of composting is simply to pile up your materials as farmers have done for eons. In a city yard, though, the piles tend to spread out and demand too much space. An enclosure or bin helps keep the material contained and speeds up the decomposition process. Ideally, a compost bin should be no more than 3 to 4 feet deep because you need to turn the material periodically, and if it's too tall it can be difficult to fork over for the average-sized or smaller person. The perimeter of the bin may vary in size depending on how much material you

Tightwad Gardening Tip

There are two household byproducts that can go straight into garden soil:

1 Coffee grounds contain fairly high amounts of nitrogen, and because they are finely ground they'll mix directly into garden soil.

2 Wood ash from a fireplace contains some phosphorous and potassium, which helps root and flower development in plants. Bits of charcoal also keep soil open and well drained. Wood ash is a caustic barrier to soft-bodied critters that won't cross over it, as well. Use wood ash to surround tender seedlings until they grow beyond the reach of plant eaters.

expect to have. They typically average 4 by 6 feet, but this is just for estimating because there are no specific dimensions except those of the lumber or block used to create the walls.

In order to get the entire mass of organic matter to decompose into compost you'll have to turn or stir it now and then. This allows surface material to move deeper where it "cooks" more thoroughly. Old-time gardeners discovered that if they had two bins side by side, they could fork all the material over from one side into the other, putting the surface stuff at the bottom in the second bin. Then later on they would repeat the process in reverse.

The least expensive enclosure, which isn't pretty but it works quite well, uses woven wire fencing you can buy in a roll at a home improvement store. The smaller the mesh the less material will work its way through and the tidier your pile will be. If all you can find is wide mesh, then use two layers slightly offset so that the holes are smaller. You can recycle a chainlink fence but bolt cutters are required to cut the fence to the right dimensions. Other types of wire include livestock fencing or chicken wire, both of which can be salvaged on the cheap from junkyards, farms, or fencing company remnants.

Don't skimp on the corner posts because they are the important structural elements. Wood posts in soil and surrounded by damp, decomposing organic matter won't last long. Instead, invest in pressure treated lumber or recycled plastic lumber posts to give you a strong, longlasting support. Other choices for much larger compost bins include railroad ties and telephone poles; both are usually treated to discourage decomposition. Create the rest of the structure with wood connectors securely nailed in

Every home in America with enough space would benefit from a space like this one smartly devoted to the creation of compost and leaf mold. This tidy area is visually separated from the rest of the garden by now-dormant hedges. It contains a large leaf mold bin to turn this usually discarded resource into vital soil-building material. There is a squat compost bin as well. Beside that is a salvaged dresser drawer used to hold garden and home refuse until it can be divided into various applications.

place, then staple the wire mesh to each side panel. The front can have a side panel or it can be left open to make it easier to dump wheelbarrow loads directly into the heap.

For more ambitious gardeners with a few more dollars to spend, the most durable compost bins are made of concrete block or stacked railroad ties. Ties are so heavy they stack well and if you offset the corners like Lincoln Logs, they will hold together just like a log cabin, without any connections. They can also be drilled and linked with metal pipe or rebar (steel reinforcement bar) pounded through the layers into the ground.

Approximately 72 percent of the waste currently being sent to landfills or incinerated consists of materials that could be put to higher and better use through recycling or composting. Most of this material is office paper, cardboard, nonrecyclable paper, and food waste.
— Minnesota Office of Environmental Assistance,
2002 The Solid Waste Policy Report

Green Choices

Many strict organic gardeners shy away from using recycled railroad ties for raised beds and compost bins. This is because in their former life, the ties were treated with creosote and other chemicals to prevent rot. The chance of these chemicals gradually leaching into the soil or compost is slight, but it's enough of a concern that some hesitate to use them. However, they are an excellent resources created out of valuable trees that should be reused, but perhaps in a non-food producing section of the garden.

*LEFT This simple, two-bin compost pile is easy to create using 2x4s and small-mesh chicken wire. Two bins allow you to fork the contents of one bin to the other, an easier way to turn compost. **CENTER** It's easy to create a pile by simply layering house and garden refuse as it becomes available. You can shake in garden soil or other materials to speed up biotic activity. **RIGHT** You can use remnants of heavy-gauge woven wire field fencing to create a leaf corral. This enclosure can be as large or small as you wish, so it fits into what space you can devote to the process.*

How To Make Compost

There are many resources out there to help you get started composting. Be advised it takes a long time to produce usable compost, and in some climates it's not as easy as it appears. To give you a quick start, here is one way to begin that doesn't require you spend any money on additives.

When a compost pile is functioning properly, it becomes a breeding ground for important bacteria and other microorganisms that feed off organic matter and turn it into crumbly, nutrient-rich humus. Rapid decomposition will cause the center of the pile to reach temperatures around 180 degrees F., which is not enough to sterilize weed seeds. While the center is heated by microbial activity, the top, bottom, and sides stay cooler and resist decomposition. When the pile is turned, this places outer materials on the inside where it too begins decomposing.

Just how often you stir or turn the compost depends on your climate, the time of year, and average temperatures. In warm weather turn it every 2 or 3 months, or even more frequently. In cooler climates, twice a year may be adequate.

When you add to the compost pile, pack down new materials until they form a 6-inch-thick layer. Then sprinkle manure or other organic fertilizer on top and water thoroughly. It's also helpful to add a thin layer of topsoil now and then to introduce fresh microorganisms to the mix, which also speeds the process. Avoid letting the heap become too wet as that cuts off oxygen vital to proper decomposition. Push a broom handle or a piece of pipe into the center of the pile now and then to make

> **Tightwad Gardening Tip**
>
> One reason composting fell out of favor was the problem of animals (pets and wild animals) digging into the heap. This was generated by the decay of animal byproducts, meat, bones, and eggshells that rural families traditionally disposed of in the pile, which was usually located far from the house due to odors. The key to modern composting is to remain vigilant about animal byproducts in your compost to ensure there will be no "bone" of contention between you, the wildlife, or your neighbors.

You can buy stackable corners and use recycled composite lumber to create a rot-proof compost bin any size you wish. These connectors are versatile enough to be used anywhere for a single or double bin design.

A simple chicken-wire box is all that's needed to make leaf mold because unlike compost, this is a very lightweight material.

aeration holes that provide oxygen between forking-over times.

Remember that composting is not a quick process, nor is it an exact science. The rate of decomposition doubles for every 18-degree rise in air temperature, so it occurs much more quickly in summer. In the South the average heap usually takes about six months while in the North up to two years may be required before it matures into usable compost.

Waste Into Wealth

It would be so much more efficient if our kitchen garbage disposal was routed right to the compost pile because that's where so much of the good stuff ends up. But the problem is that all waste is not equal, and the art of composting is to know what is suitable for the heap and what must be thrown into the landfill. Above all, remember that what does get composted will work better if it's in smaller pieces, so rather than a whole banana peel, chop it up into a few pieces before adding to the compost. And nothing composted from the house or garden should include stems any larger in diameter than a pencil.

Do Not Add These To the Compost Pile
- Oak, holly, magnolia, or conifer leaves — these do not decompose.
- Toxic plants such as poison oak or ivy.
- Plants with large thorns — unless the thorns are removed first.
- Wood byproducts treated with chemicals.
- Metals of any kind, and glass.
- Aggressive weeds that sprout from their roots such as runner grasses.
- Animal byproducts, including fats or oils, bones, hair, or pet manures.
- Diseased or insect-infested plant parts.
- Toxic substances.

Leaf Mold Is Fast And Free

If you've ever moved a pile of leaves that sat all winter and found the bottom layer turned into a dark crumbly substance, then you've met leaf mold. It's an old-time gardener's "black gold" to be added into everything from vegetable gardens to potting soil.

Leaf mold is the lazy gardener's compost because it's easy to make and ready to use far sooner than compost. Plus, you make it all at once in fall. Leaf mold does not contain the high nutrient content of compost, but it's a fine soil improver that can be enhanced by fertilizers. Leaves are plentiful in autumn and it's far easier to recycle them into your garden than try to stuff them into bags for the landfill.

Leaf mold is made in a corral, which is simply a loose wire fence set in a circle that allows you to fill it to the top with leaves. You can make as many corrals as you wish, depending on how many leaves are available. Here's how:

Obtain a length of woven wire fence 3 to 4 feet tall and long enough to make an enclosure about 4 to 8 feet in diameter. If you have very few leaves, make the circle only a few feet across. Secure it into a corral ring with wire and stake it to stand up stiffly on its own.

When the leaves start to fall, rake them up and throw them in the corral. When the first layer is about a foot deep, wet it down. Then turn on some lively music, don your work boots, and hop inside. Stomp the leaves down into a tight layer.

Top each layer with a thin covering of soil, and scatter any organic fertilizer you have along with it. If you have chickens or rabbits, their manure is ideal.

The next time you rake leaves, put another foot-deep layer in the corral and have another go at it. Get the kids involved, too. Repeat the process until the corral is as full as you can get it. In warmer climates, the leaf mold might be ready by late spring, but farther north you can expect it to mature by summer's end.

Tightwad Gardening Tip

Never harvest sand or ground shells from coastal beaches if it is to be used in the soil or around plants. This material contains high amounts of salts that can leach into the soil to alter its pH. This is particularly important with acid-soil-loving plants such as rhododendrons. If you must use rocks and shells collected from the beach in your garden décor, soak and rinse them a few times in fresh water before placing in the garden.

Tightwad Gardening Tip

For an inexpensive way to shred autumn leaves for compost heaps without spending much money, you'll need a rotary lawn mower with a catcher bag. Rake up your leaves and spread them into a low or flat-top pile a few inches thick. With the catcher bag attached, simply mow the pile and the leaves will be chopped to medium texture and neatly deposited in the bag. Pour these into your compost or leaf mold bin and repeat.

PART TWO

Environmental Cents

THE "NEW" EMPHASIS ON GOING "GREEN" ISN'T REALLY NEW;
it's just another trend based on concerns of global warming, waste, and
an ever-shrinking world. The rise of organic produce and ordinary products
created in ways that have less impact on the environment inevitably leads to
higher prices for these green choices. But, just as this movement got moving,
the global economic crisis caused some serious changes in our income and
spending habits. Higher prices for green products may simply no longer be
within one's budget despite a dedication to living a greener lifestyle.

This part of the book is dedicated to all those who long to live green but
can't afford to buy green. It is designed to utilize old and new ideas to reduce
all unnecessary spending. It may prove yet to be the best road to a really
great "green" garden. Because environmental "cents" makes environmental
"sense."

4 Nature's Climate Control:
Saving energy dollars.

Ours is the most wasteful nation on Earth. We waste more energy than we import. With about the same standard of living, we use twice as much energy per person as do other countries like Germany, Japan, and Sweden.
— Jimmy Carter, 39th President of the United States, Address to the Nation, April 18, 1977

When the great energy crisis gripped America in the 1970s, the notion of energy conservation as we know it was born. With sky-high prices, everyone sought ways to reduce heating and cooling bills. Energy conservation was the buzzword, whether it was using less gasoline in a big car or finding ways to conserve heating oil in a leaky old house. Today, there is a new layer added to this financial burden: one of the global ecology and global warming. For those concerned about the environment, excessive energy use isn't just expensive, it's wasteful. If our natural resources are to sustain us as long as possible, everyone must learn to conserve.

For most folks, all the talk about alternative energies, energy-efficient construction, and green materials is just talk because it takes money to put these ideas into action. Replacing windows in an old house, adding more insulation, or any of a dozen other strategies for keeping our homes comfortable in order to use less energy can require a second mortgage to accomplish. Fortunately, some scientists have devoted themselves to creating options for the "little people" that don't cost an arm and a leg.

For gardeners, those techniques that utilize landscaping for energy conservation are the most affordable solutions. They allow the structure of a house to remain the same while changing the way we plant to counter extremes of climate, naturally.

Your Goal: Maximize Summer Shade

Solar radiation is simply heat from the sun. It can fall on your home or it can bathe outdoor areas of any kind: paved, wild, or landscaped. Sunlight and its heat-generating abilities can be pleasant in the cool season, but in summer sunshine becomes the enemy of indoor comfort. It can also cause outdoor spaces to become unusually warm depending on the kind of materials it falls onto. Some of these, such as paving, actually absorb and hold heat, then release it gradually after dark. It's this factor that makes our urban environment hotter at night than the surrounding open space, a phenomenon known as a "heat island."

City planners discovered this problem decades ago and sought to reduce it in new communities by adding trees

The olive tree shading this desert home grows lush in summer; then the canopy is thinned in winter to let the sun shine in.

for shade, particularly where there are large areas of paving such as parking lots and boulevards. Shaded paving does not grow so hot during the day. Not only do cars parked under shade stay cooler, a city is more attractive, air quality improves, and the heat island effect is reduced. A cooler city means less energy consumption is needed to make the residents comfortable. Best of all, creating shade doesn't cost a cent beyond the initial investment in trees.

If we take what scientists, architects, and planners have learned about cooling cities and apply it to our own homesites, the same effect occurs. In fact, it can have far more impact because you have total control of what you plant and where. In the Hot Zone, the need for shade is a primary consideration because this makes outdoor living more comfortable and assists an air conditioner in summer.

Your home receives this direct solar radiation and, depending on the type of exterior building material you have, the walls will absorb and reflect this heat to a greater or lesser degree. Perhaps the best example of this is demonstrated by a car sitting in the sun on a cold day with all the windows rolled up. The heat passing through the glass is sufficient to warm the interior of the car. This also happens through building windows and walls, which can transfer heat to the interior of your house. Double-pane windows and heavy wall insulation are two ways to reduce this problem, but they are expensive solutions.

Creating shade to appear in the right place, in the right season, and at the right time of day is what energy conservation landscaping is all about. Solar radiation that falls on plants is absorbed into the leaves and utilized in the process of photosynthesis. Therefore, well-placed trees function in two ways when they encounter solar radiation. First, they literally consume the energy into their cells and use it in this natural process. Second, they intercept it before it reaches hard surfaces such as paving, windows, or building walls. Unlike hard surfaces, leaves do not hold heat for long. They quickly release heat energy as soon as the surrounding temperatures begin to drop.

Studies show that a single mature shade tree can equal 10,999 BTUs of cooling by shading and absorbing solar radiation; homeowners can expect to save hundreds of dollars in annual air-conditioning costs. In fact, some trees are so vital to a home's interior comfort that losing an "old friend" in a storm can have

Follow the Sun to Cash in on Solar Power

Even the most perfectly designed passive solar home can be spoiled by improper landscaping. No passive solar home can be a cookie cutter design because each must be properly oriented toward the four cardinal directions to obtain the highest energy efficiency. It's so important, the architect often guides the client with landscape design to ensure the solar benefits are maximized.

Passive solar also applies to landscaping. If your homesite is planted properly, even an ordinary home with no passive solar design elements can enjoy some benefits from solar landscaping. (That means dollars in your pocket that won't go to the electric company while you remain cool and comfortable all summer long—or warm and toasty all winter!)

To cash in on passive solar landscaping benefits, you must look at your house and its orientation to the sun. This is the key to everything else, and it is non-negotiable. Passive solar homes are designed so that a long side is facing south. This is the most important exposure because in winter the sun is lower in the southern sky and this gives you the direct impact of the sun's rays to windows on that side. In summer the sun moves farther to the north, passing more directly overhead. At that time of year the southern side receives no direct sunlight. The sun's rays are concentrated on the east side in the morning and on the roof at noon, when attic fans kick in to cool. In the afternoon, the west side of the house heats up in the setting sun. That's why every solar home must be designed individually for its own lot so that the orientation to the four corners of the compass is accurately met.

This orientation relates to the landscape too, particularly when it comes to planting trees. Planting deciduous shade trees around passive solar homes can enhance their energy conservation ability. While these trees offer much-wanted shade in summer when they are in full leaf, when they lose their leaves in fall it allows direct solar exposure during the winter. Even if you do not have a passive solar house, the value of deciduous trees remains equally important. Studies have documented that much energy is saved when trees work with your house's design to keep you more comfortable.

Shaded houses use 2.0 kilowatt hours per square foot, per year; unshaded houses use 3.3 KWH.

One tree absorbs the same amount of BTUs in a day as five air conditioners running for 20 hours use.

Walls shaded by trees are generally 15 degrees F. cooler than unshaded walls. Even shading your outdoor air conditioning unit or evaporative cooler increases the efficiency and the life of your equipment.

far more long-reaching financial consequences than you might expect.

The cooling effects of landscaping aren't limited just to trees. Bare earth acts much like paving by absorbing solar heat; it gets hot, but reflects a bit less into the atmosphere. The areas

How To Recognize A Solar-Friendly Tree

Summer

Solar-friendly trees are deciduous, meaning they lose their leaves in fall and grow them again in spring. Deciduous trees provide shade during the heat of summer, then remain bare during winter to allow light to shine through their branches.

Tree species that lose their leaves in early fall and grow them again in late spring maximize the time they remain bare during winter. In cold climates direct solar exposure is important early in the season, and if spring comes late, you don't need increased shade while it's still chilly outside.

Winter

Even after a tree has lost its leaves, the density of its twigs and branches in the canopy can still block sunlight. Canopy density varies with each species, from around 25 percent to as much as 80 percent. The average density is around 40 percent. A solar-friendly tree should have an open branching pattern, but existing trees with dense branching can be made "friendlier" by carefully thinning their canopy. Seedpods and catkins that remain on trees during winter increase canopy density, as do tenacious leaves that may not detach as readily in some milder climates. Solar-friendly trees should have no parts that linger.

adjacent to bare dirt or paving can make the surrounding spaces even hotter than the ambient temperatures nearby. But the same surface planted in grass or groundcover will radiate a fraction of that heat. A great deal of heat energy is absorbed and then dissipated into the earth, rendering the adjacent spaces far cooler. It's easy to see why the fewer paved surfaces and the more green foliage you plant around the house, the less summer's hot temperatures will affect you. The exception, of course, is paving already shaded by a tree canopy that never receives direct solar exposure.

Passive Solar Pluses

"Passive solar" is a term used by architects to describe building designs that take advantage of the sun without special mechanisms. The designs are truly passive in that they do not involve any expensive or finicky panels, equipment, wiring, or piping. The architects adapted some lessons learned from nature and utilized them in a positive way to make our homes warmer in

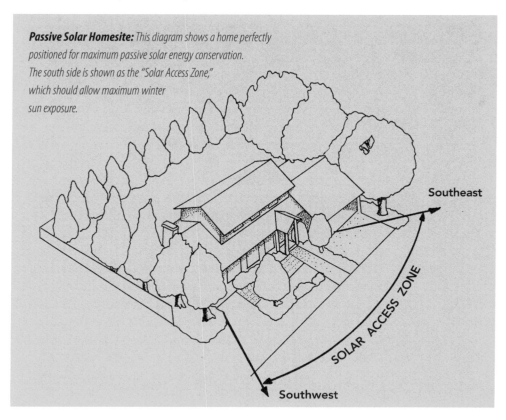

Passive Solar Homesite: This diagram shows a home perfectly positioned for maximum passive solar energy conservation. The south side is shown as the "Solar Access Zone," which should allow maximum winter sun exposure.

Southeast

SOLAR ACCESS ZONE

Southwest

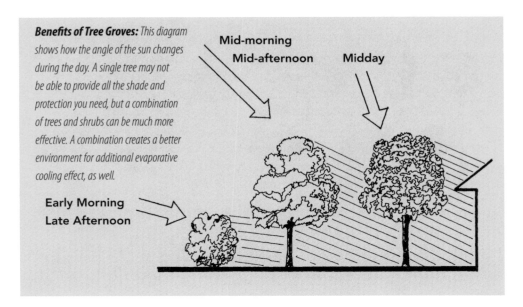

Benefits of Tree Groves: *This diagram shows how the angle of the sun changes during the day. A single tree may not be able to provide all the shade and protection you need, but a combination of trees and shrubs can be much more effective. A combination creates a better environment for additional evaporative cooling effect, as well.*

Mid-morning
Mid-afternoon
Midday
Early Morning
Late Afternoon

winter and cooler in summer. Just go back to the car window analogy to understand what they try to do. Homes that are built with such designs from the ground up are remarkably comfortable year-round.

Green Choices

In the past, raking fall leaves was considered a waste of time. Today, the green home benefits from its own crop of organic matter that can be recycled into compost or leaf mold. Add that to energy savings and deciduous trees become doubly green!

Testing For Accurate Patterns

To get a better idea of exactly where to plant a tree for optimal passive-solar design, you need to know where the shadow will fall. The shadow pattern is the size and angle of shade cast by a tree (or anything else) during the hot summer months.

A simple method of determining the shadow pattern acts like the needle on a sundial, which will tell you exactly where a shadow will fall during summer. This can only be done in summer when the sun is as far north in the sky as it will be throughout the year. Here's how: Obtain a long pole and anchor it in the ground where you think a tree should be planted. Then watch its shadow pattern throughout the day to see exactly where the shadows fall in the morning, at noon, and in the evening. (This is also a

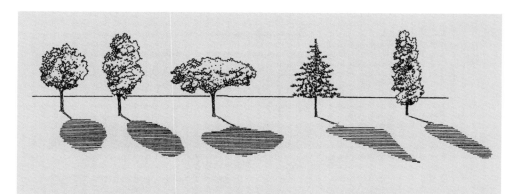

Each species of tree has a certain form that will be reflected in the size and shape of its shadow pattern. This is a must-know detail for selecting a solar-friendly tree. Sometimes the more unusual shapes are ideal on small lots, where you must accurately place trees in order to avoid shading your neighbors' sunny southern side. Left to Right: round, vertical oval, horizontal oval, pyramidal, columnar

great lesson on learning how the sun moves across the sky over the course of the day; if the pole remains in place long enough, you'll also learn how summer and winter affects sun exposures in your garden.)

Another trick to determine how tall a tree must be in order to shade a particular area is commonly used by architects to see how the height or mass of a proposed building fits into its immediate surroundings. To start, you need a perfectly calm day. Then fill a large balloon with helium and tie it to a roll of kite string. Anchor the string to the ground where you think a tree should be planted. As the sun rises and sets, the place where the balloon's shadow falls tells you how tall a tree you need. Then match your finding with a suitable deciduous tree that fits into the space available and you'll have the perfect passive-solar solution. To test more than one location or to evaluate the needed width of a potential tree, use two or more balloons. Then be sure to turn the balloons over to the kids when you're through.

Picking The Right Tree for Energy Conservation

Not all trees have the same form or silhouette. A tree used for solar shading must have a broad canopy, like an open umbrella, rather than one that is columnar, like a baseball bat. Obviously, the umbrella-shaped tree will give you far more shading for your money.

Above all, trees must be able to survive in your climate zone and should be resistant both to pests and diseases. Some, such as the American elm, have been decimated by pests. Some very fast-growing species such as many poplars tend to have a shorter-than-average lifespan. Avoid all of the invasively rooted species such as willows, poplars, maples, and alders if you live on a small lot.

Choose your trees carefully if you live in a smaller homesite where limited shading is needed. They will be among the most visible plants around a home so they should be attractive and possibly offer fall color. Any tree should be capable of intercepting direct sunlight and absorbing heat before it can reach the walls and windows of a home. It should also be tall enough to shade a portion of the roof.

Climbing roses, shrubs, and vines help lend greater insulation to historic structures, which are notorious for poor insulation.

These are just a few considerations for selecting the best tree or trees for your homesite. Because choices vary considerably from coast to coast, it pays to consult an agent from your local agricultural cooperative extension or ask a Master Gardener to help you out. These experts keep up to date with the latest tree news so you can "weed out" all the unsuitable candidates first.

Trees and all green plants are beneficial to your environment because they transpire, which is how a tree "breathes." In this process a tree takes in carbon dioxide and releases oxygen. When trees are planted together in groves, humidity and oxygen surrounding them accumulates, adding yet another benefit in dry climates: evaporative cooling. This cooling effect is minimal when only one tree is present or when trees are widely spaced. By using groves of trees to shade your home, you can help reduce the ambient

Using Vines For Exterior Insulation

It's difficult to add insulation to the interior walls of an older home, but there is a less expensive way to reduce radiant heat gain and loss through the walls. Just add insulation to the *outside* by planting vines. These can be trained to cover your house walls evenly. Its shading effect is considerable, and the dead air spaces between the vine foliage and the exterior wall is also a very effective insulator. Taller shrubs planted up against a house also provide the same benefits of shade and insulation.

The simplest way to insulate walls with vines is to choose species that cling to the surfaces. The downside of this idea is repainting; plus, the vines themselves can cause all sorts of unseen structural damage if they're not controlled. Vines that do not cling can be espaliered onto a simple grid trellis bolted to the house wall. Before painting, detach the trellis, or untie the vine from the trellis and allow it to flop over onto the ground. Then tie it back up again when you're through painting.

Vines are an old technique for shading windowpanes from

This traditional Spanish home features the practice of shading windows by training small vines to grow over the top.

direct overhead exposure. This is popular in the warm climates of the Mediterranean and Latin America. Roses or bougainvillea are grown to drape over the tops of the windows where they grow thick and luxurious enough to cast a considerable shadow.

Draping windows and doorways with vine bowers is simpler than covering entire walls by a blanket of leaves. The key is to create anchors in the house wall to have something to tie to. It's vital to keep the vines thinned, removing old runners so new ones can take their place. This eliminates dead wood and interior leaf buildup and keeps them flowering heavily all year long.

In a warm climate a creeping fig is one of the best clinging vines due to its very small, dense leaves. It produces a secondary type of foliage shown here that is much larger and coarser, that adds greater insulating ability, but this is usually sheared off.

This cable is stretched by turnbuckles to keep it tight under the increasing weight of a young wisteria vine. Such supports make it much easier to repair or paint in the future rather than using nails pounded into the siding or a rigid trellis.

Densely Growing Vines Suitable for Wall Insulation

Botanical Name	Common Name	Evergreen	Clings	Hardy
Euonymus fortunei 'Colorata'	Winter Creeper	yes	yes	yes
Doxantha ungus-cati	Cat's Claw Creeper	yes	yes	no
Ficus pumila	Creeping Fig	yes	yes	no
Hedera helix	English Ivy	yes	yes	yes
Parthenocissus triscuspidata	Boston Ivy	no	yes	yes
Parthenocissus quinquefolia	Virginia Creeper	no	yes	yes
Wisteria sinensis	Wisteria	no	no	yes

Showy Flowering Vines for Draping Over Windows

Botanical Name	Common Name	Evergreen	Hardy	Fragrant	Color
Bougainvillea hybrids	Bougainvillea	yes	no	no	varies
Campsis radicans	Trumpet Creeper	no	yes	no	red
Gelsemium sempervirens	Carolina Jessamine	yes	no	no	yellow
Hydrangea anomala	Creeping Hydrangea	no	yes	no	white
Jasminum polyanthum	Chinese Jasmine	yes	no	yes	white
Lonicera spp.	Honeysuckle	yes	no	yes	varies
Tecomaria capensis	Cape Honeysuckle	yes	no	no	orange

While dwarf forms of English ivy make a lovely evergreen cloak for an exposed wall, the way this plant clings can cause serious structural damage. The rootlets shown here invade mortar and cause it to disintegrate with time and the mortar is easily dislodged when the rootlets are removed.

Cold Zone Basics

Goal: *Reduce winter winds; increase heat conservation.*

It is not difficult to understand how wind affects ambient temperatures in cold climates. The effect can be so great that temperatures are adjusted for "wind chill" in weather reports. On a typical 20-degree day, for example, the temperature will drop with each 5-mile-per-hour increase in wind speed. The wind chill factor is critical in determining the amount of energy required to heat a household during winter.

The reason that down comforters are so warm is that downy feathers create dead air spaces that present a barrier against the loss of body heat. The value of goose down is that it remains fluffy, which helps support these air spaces inside each quilted cell of stuffing. But if down becomes wet, the fluff collapses and virtually all the insulation value is lost. Double-pane windows work on the down principal. They have a layer of dead air sandwiched between the two sheets of glass. This dead air space is a valuable insulating barrier between areas of varying temperatures.

The deciduous Boston ivy, Parthenocissus tricuspidata, *is shown here in spring as it is leafing out. When leaves are absent for winter it is easy to control growth. This vine allows south-facing walls to absorb winter heat while shading them in summer.*

Take this dead-air concept and apply it to a homesite. A barrier of dead air around your house will insulate its walls from direct contact with cold wind. Think of wind as you would water to better understand how it will impact your home. Wind cannot blow through your house so it must go around the sides. This

Tightwad Gardening Tip

Never allow a vine to grow beyond the reach of your ladder. Being out of reach is how vines get a reputation of being unmanageable. If you can't reach them, you can't control them.

forces more direct contact with walls and windows on the sides that do not face wind head on. In many cases the wind will eddy and swirl in many directions, which increases access to cracks in the walls or windows. You can wrap your home in evergreen foundation plantings or trained vines, which provide dead air space to create a sizeable insulation blanket.

To plant for energy conservation, you must know how the prevailing winds and storm winds differ with each season. To find out, make a poor man's weather vane. Simply pound a tall stake or pole into the ground so it is sturdy enough to stand up to the wind. Then tie strips of brightly colored cloth or ribbon securely to the stake at two-foot intervals. When the wind blows, the direction of the ribbons tell you how the wind blows overhead and closer to the earth where plants grow.

In order to block wind on a larger scale for energy conservation and to make outdoor spaces more comfortable, you must arrange a barrier of trees called a "windbreak." A windbreak is basically a row of tightly spaced trees arranged in a line that runs perpendicular to the prevailing direction of the wind. If there is a gap in the windbreak, the wind will be channeled through this opening, as if it were a wind tunnel, and the wind speed can actually increase.

Windbreaks can be designed on a smaller scale for suburban homes. The key is to create a barrier of plants that runs across the prevailing direction of winter storm winds. Windbreaks are usually composed of evergreen trees and shrubs for continuous protection in every season.

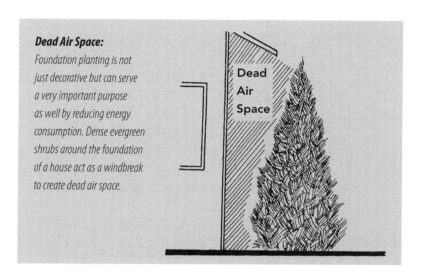

Dead Air Space: *Foundation planting is not just decorative but can serve a very important purpose as well by reducing energy consumption. Dense evergreen shrubs around the foundation of a house act as a windbreak to create dead air space.*

Dead
Air
Space

Trees and Shrubs to Block Cold Winds

Windbreaks can also help create sun-drenched spaces of relatively dead air outdoors. If you live on a small lot, you may decide reducing cold winds not only keeps your house warmer in winter, it also creates a sheltered area to visit between seasons. But don't feel you need a big windbreak to make a difference. A single, well-placed evergreen tree or shrub, or even a small hedge, can have a big effect.

Windbreaks need not be restricted to trees. Shrub windbreaks are highly effective at protecting your house from the onslaught of icy winter winds. Shrubs don't grow so tall that they block the sun from reaching the windowpanes, either. But they can be large enough to change the wind pattern or reduce its velocity to make the house and the spaces around it far more comfortable. Shrubs used as a windbreak can also do a great job in filling gaps beneath trees that have grown so tall they no longer have enough low branches to block the wind on a pedestrian level.

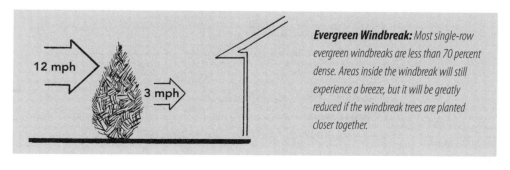

12 mph

3 mph

Evergreen Windbreak: *Most single-row evergreen windbreaks are less than 70 percent dense. Areas inside the windbreak will still experience a breeze, but it will be greatly reduced if the windbreak trees are planted closer together.*

Always keep your neighbor's solar needs in mind. If you plant a windbreak, it may eventually provide unwanted shade next door. Likewise, your neighbor's windbreak could shade the south side of your house and destroy the benefits of solar-friendly landscaping. The worst case scenario would be that your trees begin to shade a neighbor's solar panels.

A tree windbreak can be no more than 70 percent dense compared to a masonry wall barrier that is 100 percent dense. With trees, 30 percent of the wind still passes through the foliage, reducing the wind speeds on the lee side of the barrier by 60 to 75 percent.

Shelterbelts

As far back as 1789, Mennonite farmers from Germany immigrated to the Russian steppes and there began to plant large windbreaks several rows thick around their fields to thwart the merciless wind. Today there are thousands of miles of these ancient, dense windbreaks protecting millions of acres of Russian farmland.

European immigrants who settled the American Great Plains brought this knowledge with them and it would become a lifesaver in this raw, open country. These super-windbreaks created both with deciduous and evergreen trees also depend largely on shrubs to create a wider, denser barrier. It is far more effective than a single windrow, but it demands more space as well.

From the start farmers planted seedlings in the virgin land, seedlings that would one day grow large enough to reduce wind erosion, protect homes, and encourage winter crop production. These arrangements, called "shelterbelts," are most successful in protecting homesites on the prairie where the icy winds are

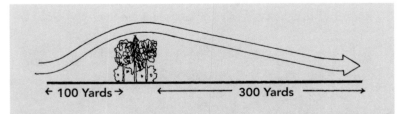

← 100 Yards →   ←————— 300 Yards —————→

Shelterbelt: *Wind speed is slowed for 100 yards on the windward side of a 30-foot-tall shelterbelt. It also slows wind up to 300 yards downwind from a shelterbelt. This illustrates how a mature shelterbelt can cause profound changes in air movement over very large areas.*

persistent. They are also effective in coastal communities, which must contend with brutal onshore breezes.

Shelterbelts encounter wind on the outside or windward side, while the lee side remains relatively calm. The speed of wind entering a shelterbelt is slowed as it bounces around inside, and by the time it exits the lee side there is very little energy left. A well-planted space between a shelterbelt and a house becomes less turbulent. Shelterbelts are also very effective at controlling snowdrift. The lee edge should be located 20 to 60 feet from a building wall for the best results.

Locating and sizing shelterbelts for a larger piece of property should be carefully considered. Factors such as wind speed, local landforms, and snowdrift must all be taken into consideration. For free advice on larger properties, contact the Natural Resource Conservation Office, a department of the USDA dedicated to soil conservation and other environmental concerns. You can also discuss the project with state or county agricultural officials, farm advisors, or university extension agents.

Most shelterbelts consist of very hardy, strong-branching, wind-resistant trees, although some flowering specimens can be planted for visual interest. The anatomy of a typical shelterbelt consists of three staggered rows, but more can be added if desired to make it less rigid in form. Smaller shrubs on the outer windward side of a shelterbelt help deflect wind upward so that some of its energy goes over the top of the barrier rather than through it.

This basic anatomy of shelterbelts helps you distribute plants in their most efficient arrangement:

Row 1 *Tall, fast-growing deciduous trees on the lee side.*
Row 2 *Evergreen trees, usually conifers, in the middle.*
Row 3 *Combination of shrubs and small trees on the outside.*

Trees and shrubs typically used in shelterbelts are planted in small sizes so they will root and become well anchored in the soil. Since they must sustain very heavy wind loads in their early years, they require sufficient rooting to stand up to the strain. Trees with rootballs the shape of a nursery container take more time to develop a strong rooting network or taproot than a bare-root plant.

The ideal small-sized tree is easily obtained in quantity from

Online Links for Windbreaks and Shelterbelts

American Forests	www.americanforests.com
Natural Resources Conservation Service	www.nrcs.usda.gov
Kelly Tree Farm	www.windbreaktrees.com

tree farms, which grow huge numbers of seedlings for farmers and reforestation projects. Growers will send you a catalog or availability list of exactly what they have in stock. You'll be surprised at how inexpensive trees are when field grown in such large numbers, particularly when they can be shipped directly to your home. In fact, growers even sell evergreens bare root in season, which eliminates the extra cost of a pot, soil, or burlap.

To plant very large windbreaks and shelterbelts, rent a trenching machine so you don't have to dig so many individual holes, particularly in hard soils. Actual spacing between rows and individual trees and shrubs will vary, so it's best to consult a professional familiar with local conditions before you buy or begin digging.

Species for Windbreaks and Shelterbelts
This list of trees and shrubs that are especially suited to windbreaks and shelterbreaks is derived from extensive research by the National Resource Conservation Service, a division of the USDA.

Botanical Name	Common Name	Height (ft.)	Spacing (ft.)
+Acer spp.	Maples	25–90	4
Amelanchier alnifolia	Saskatoon	20	4
+Caragana arborescens	Siberian Pea Tree	18	4
Carpinus betulus	European Hornbeam	60	4
Cornus mas	Carnelian Cherry	24	4
Crataegus phaenophyrum	Washington Hawthorne	30	4
+Eleagnus angustifolia	Russian Olive	30	4
*Eucalyptus spp.	Gum Tree	100	6

Botanical Name	Common Name	Height (ft.)	Spacing (ft.)
Forsythia intermedia	Forsythia	9	4
+Fraxinus pennsylvanica	Green Ash	60	6
+*Juniperus communis	Common Juniper	3–30	2
Ligustrum amurense	Amur Privet	15	2
*Ligustrum japonicum	Japanese Privet	6–18	3
+Lonicera tatarica	Tatarian Honeysuckle	9	3
+Maclura pomifera	Osage Orange	60	6
*Picea abies	Norway Spruce	100	6
+*Picea glauca	White Spruce	90	6
+*Picea pungens	Colorado Blue Spruce	90	6
*Pinus banksiana	Jack Pine	75	4
*Pinus nigra	Austrian Pine	90	6
*Pinus strobus	White Pine	100	6
+*Pinus sylvestris	Scotch Pine	70	6
+Populus spp.	Poplar, Cottonwood	50–100	4
+Prunus virginiana	Chokecherry	30	4
Quercus imbricaria	Shingle Oak	75	12
+Quercus macrocarpa	Burr Oak	75	12
+Salix alba	White Willow	75	6
Viburnum prunifolium	Blackhaw	15	3
Viburnum sieboldi	Siebold Viburnum	30	4

* Indicates evergreen.

+ Indicates rugged and hardy species suitable for Great Plains shelterbelts.

Spp. indicates many species of this genus are suitable.

5 Never Thirsty:
Cut your water bill in half.

Almost all the things we do with water require less water than we use to do them. I think improving efficiency is the most important tool in our arsenal. Let's do more with less water—grow more food, flush more toilets, wash more clothes—do more of everything with less.
— Peter Gleick, President, Pacific Institute

Drought-tolerant landscaping used to be restricted to homes in the Southwestern states where water conservation has always been a serious issue. But today, with dwindling resources, regional droughts, and growing demand on water supplies, water conservation is everyone's concern. Like all products, high demand and limited supply drive prices higher, and water is no exception. Now it has become something that actually has an impact on our finances, and that should be recognized by every budget-minded gardener.

In order to save water and lower your bills, you should always be aware of how much water is being used or wasted in the garden. In fact, there's an important relationship between how we water and how drought tolerant a plant will ultimately be. So for the sake of our children and the environment, paying attention to water conservation is one of the most vital green issues around; we must heighten our awareness of all water use, both indoors and out.

Earth and Water

The key to getting started in water conservation is to understand the basic relationship of water to soil. In order to know the most efficient way of getting water to the roots of thirsty plants and nowhere else, we have to know how water behaves in and around soils. The following terms and their definitions are vital to understanding this chapter, which is built upon these concepts.

Percolation rate: Percolation rate is the speed at which water is absorbed by the soil. Water percolates instantly through porous sandy soil. But, it is very slow to percolate through dense clay soils. This dictates that we should apply water differently for each soil type.

Surface evaporation: The surface of the soil contains moisture that gradually evaporates into the atmosphere. In hot, dry climates the evaporation speed doubles. If evaporation is checked, little moisture is lost to the air and the rest remains available to plants for a much longer time within the soil.

Root zone: The root zone is the area of underground soil that is accessed by a plant's root system. A plant cannot draw moisture from anywhere else but this vital zone, so keeping moisture there is a primary goal.

Water shortages aren't limited to the West anymore. This Delaware garden utilizes beautiful perennials from cooler, arid regions of the world to cut back on household consumption.

The combination of Mexican feather grass (Nassella tenuissima) and a midwestern native prickly pear (Opuntia humifusa) offer great diversity in drought-resistant gardens.

Deep rooting: Plants are more able to survive drought if they develop deep roots that can reach moisture trapped far under-ground. This is vital to maximizing the drought resistance of a plant. But if a plant is encouraged to root on the surface (through shallow watering), even a famously drought-resistant species may lose this quality altogether.

Drought-Tolerant Plants

Drought-tolerant plants originate in climates that experience a long dry season or extended seasons of periodic drought. The plants indigenous to these climates have evolved coping methods. For example, they may grow quickly after brief rains;

they may develop massive, deep-root systems; or their leaves may be a certain color (such as grey-green) or have a fuzzy surface that helps reduce moisture loss.

In nature, a drought-resistant plant species will begin deep rooting immediately after sprouting from seed. These early deep roots, which can reach three feet deep, are there to get a plant through the first dry season. But when that same species is grown in a container, its roots hit the bottom of the container very soon. Plus, its roots can't extend outward, either. So when your new drought-tolerant plant goes into the garden, it's not really drought tolerant—yet. It can take up to two years for roots to grow out and down to begin their natural hunt for moisture. The way you water and the depth to which the soil is saturated during those first two years contributes heavily to the ultimate size of a plant's root zone.

Green Choices

Think twice before you switch out all your garden plants for less thirsty species. The resources to grow all the new plants, the waste from the plants that were removed from the garden, and the transportation used to do it all may cost more in dollars and resources than you'll ultimately save from watering less. It's far better to figure out where the major water wasters are, such as the lawn or growing cutting roses, and swap them out for something a little less thirsty.

A Gallery of Water Conservative Landscapes

Water conservative gardens often feature truly exotic succulents that offer year-round color, texture, and variety.

Sicilian sweet pea (Lathyrus odoratus 'Cupani') with blue fescue and snow-in-summer (Cerastium tomentosum) combined with Agave americana.

Low Pressure Irrigation

When water is in short supply, traditional spray sprinkler systems are far too inefficient to be sustainable. This is partly because fine mists of water are vulnerable to evaporation and can be blown off course by the wind. The drip system prevents this problem by delivering water to the root zones of the plants and nowhere else; the flow rates are so low that each drop soaks directly into the soil. Thus, there is little moisture lost to surface evaporation. Deep saturation of the soil encourages adventurous rooting far below the soil surface. Since drip systems function at low pressure, fittings don't have to be securely glued together, making it easy to fit it all together.

There is a newer version of this system called micro-spray that works a bit better with ornamental landscapes. It combines the visibility of a spray system with the low-flow efficiency of a drip system. It is simple to install, but there is more evaporation loss because it does spray. Its pencil-sized heads don't water as deeply as a true drip system, though. They do provide a small-scale alternative for watering groundcovers and other low, spreading plants.

You can install a drip or micro-spray system in an existing landscape, although they are not suited to large areas of lawns or groundcover. Each plant may require one or more emitters, so creativity may be required to ensure everything is adequately watered.

If a standard spray system is present, you can adapt it to a drip system, but there may be some problems with water pres-sure. The simplest way to adapt to a drip system is to replace the

Israel's Gift To An Arid World

When immigrants to Israel began to reclaim the desert, they had a very limited freshwater supply to support a growing population. Some of the greatest researchers devoted themselves to finding a more efficient use of water in agriculture. Simcha Blass utilized newly emerging plastics technology to create a simple system of delivering water to plant roots with little to no loss. It was vastly more efficient than previous systems, inexpensive, and required few special tools to install. It was centered around a newly designed emitter that controlled how water was released. Emitters are rated at gallons-per-hour compared to a traditional spray head, which is rated in gallons-per-minute. Such a change was truly revolutionary. First introduced in 1959, it proved so wildly successful that what is today called "drip irrigation" became a staple in Australia and arid regions of the Americas in the 1960s.

No New Technology Goes Unpunished

After the introduction of drip irrigation to Southern California, the highway department went into widespread implementation to reduce water consumption due to freeway landscaping. At first the systems were fine; but then shrubs began to die, one here, another there, all over the city. Workers were sent to check the source of the problem and replace the plants. They discovered two things: First, rodents had chewed into the plastic pipes to reach water during the dry season, which caused a short of the emitters that fed shrubs farther down the line. Second, in wetter areas the emitters began to develop algae bloom. Algae would invade the emitter, forcing it open. Eventually an emitter became so packed that flow was restricted. What this story illustrates is the Achilles heel of these watering systems; you can't just turn them on and observe whether the emitters are fully functional or not. Because they are both very small and too often hidden beneath the plants, they are often forgotten. If they fail or become restricted, the plants die, which is too often the first sign of a problem. For this reason it is essential to check your system often, particularly during hot, dry months when plants are stressed by the slightest changes in water availability.

spray head with a drip system manifold cap. This is a screw-on fitting that is studded with nipples that fit easily into plastic drip system tubing. The final product can somewhat resemble an octopus. Be sure to install the emitters as indicated by the manufacturer's manual because they are essential to pressure control.

Where there is no existing system, it's simple to set up a drip irrigation system by setting up drip lines from a nearby hose bib. With low-flow systems, you can serve many more plants on a single line than a spray system.

*Because low-pressure lines are flexible and simple to assemble without special tools, virtually anyone can do it. **Left:** Plants located in rows are the easiest to water with a drip system. Allow at least one emitter per plant. **Center:** Larger trees need multiple emitters located away from the trunk but still within the outer edges of the canopy. Emitters positioned at regular intervals ensure water is delivered equally throughout the root zone. **Right:** A simple system run by an ordinary garden hose can water pots, troughs, windowboxes, and hanging baskets far more efficiently than you can with a hose, and with a lot less work!*

Green Choice
Consciousness of how you use wastewater from your kitchen is part of the new awareness of the environment. Whenever you end up with a leftover glass of water, don't pour it down the drain— take it outside and pour it into your potted plants. Though it is a small thing, it does save water and money in the long run and demonstrates a reverence for this most essential resource.

Water-Wise Watering
Amid the conveniences of modern-day living, we have developed a casual attitude about water use. If you had been born a hundred years ago and had to draw water from a well one bucket at a time, your awareness would be quite different. In fact, in the ancient gardens of desert regions most plants were grown in pots, where indoor wastewater could be readily poured into them. Just as we have become aware of recycling and reusing, so must we wake up to our wasteful patterns of water use.

If you are watering with a traditional spray system, the best way to conserve is to cut the rate at which water is delivered. Do not reduce the coverage of the sprinkler head because this will leave parts of your garden dry and the plants will die. But, slower delivery means that the soil has more time to absorb each drop, which also limits wasteful runoff. If you have dense soil or clay, this may prove better for your plants and they will thrive because water penetrates deeper.

   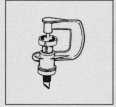

Components of a Low-pressure System:
Top Left: The "Y" filter is located close to the water source and traps sediment that could clog the small openings at each emitter. **Top Right:** Even if there is no sprinkler system currently in place, you can install a drip system off an outdoor hose bib. **Bottom Left:** This clock will turn the system on and off at a preset time each day. Some of these controllers are solar-powered; others function on a battery. You can also use a manual timer that you set for the duration you want the system to run; it will turn off later on its own just like a kitchen timer. **Bottom Right:** This detail shows the emitter of one kind of micro-spray system. It sits atop a small stake and is attached to ¼-inch lateral tubing.

A low-flow sprinkler head sprays the exact radius and pattern as its predecessor. For example, a standard spray head may deliver two gallons per minute while a low-flow system might distribute just 1 or 1.5 gallons per minute. This savings not only can cut your water bills, it will work better in soils with slow percolation rates, particularly where lawn foot traffic has caused heavy compaction. Simply remove the heads, note the kind of head that is used on each riser, and go shopping for low-flow substitutes.

Save by Avoiding These Common Mistakes

Forgotten garden hoses left running or not completely turned off will trickle unnoticed until someone uses the hose again. In some cases they may run for days before being discovered. There is an easy solution: purchase an automatic timer for each hose's bib that automatically turns off the water even if you forget.

Keep your sprinkler system in good repair. Water can leak from broken water lines, sprinkler lines, or risers, reducing efficiency and possibly delivering water where there are no plants. That affects the spray heads at the end of the line that need the water to ensure adequate coverage.

Leaking garden hoses, couplers, and hose bibs waste a lot of water. Leaks occur when the rubber parts inside a faucet deteriorate. Repair or replace with new parts when water begins seeping out just below the knob. The same thing occurs when the washers inside hose couplers are lost or fail. Keep new rubber garden hose washers on hand at all times and replace them promptly.

Poorly adjusted sprinkler heads water unplanted areas guaranteeing 100 percent runoff in those areas. Heads that are blocked by plants or weeds can also restrict delivery and cause wet spots and encourage weed growth. Be aware of the sprinkler heads at all times because poor adjustment may also short-change plants elsewhere within its coverage radius.

Watering on a schedule, especially when the soil is already moist, is not only wasteful but it's unhealthy for the plants, too. Be aware of the weather every day and adjust your automatic controller in a timely fashion. Reduce or extend watering times and turn off the watering system altogether in wet weather.

Avoid watering in the heat of the day or in windy weather. In the heat, water evaporation rates skyrocket. Wind-blown water won't fall where it should, leaving those spots in the garden overly dry. Watering very early in the morning or late evening are ideal times during the growing season.

Green Choices

Pay attention to the weather every day. Those who work in controlled environments are often unaware of what's going on outside. They fail to realize factors such as dry wind, excessive heat, and lack of rain can greatly influence plants and the amount of water they need. Become as weather aware as a farmer so you can adjust your system in a timely fashion. This not only saves resources but optimizes conditions for the plants.

Fixed Riser Sprinkler: This is how most sprinkler heads appear underground. The feeder line is constructed with a "T" fitting that supports the riser. Risers screw into the "T" whereas the other two connection points are permanently glued. If a fixed riser is run over, hit, or crushed aboveground, the impact may crack the "T" underground. If there is any sign of water, dig down to the "T" to inspect for breaks or hairline cracks, which can waste a lot of water if they go undiscovered.

Pop-Up Head on Swing Joint: This detail shows how a pop-up head functions and at what level it is set in the soil. Since these heads can be expensive, a swing joint helps to reduce impact damage.

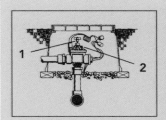 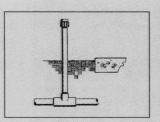 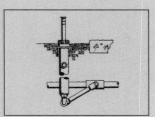

Electric Solenoid Valve : An automatically controlled sprinkler valve can be located above ground or in a valve box as shown here. There are two manual controls on this valve. The flow control is #1; it can be adjusted to allow more, or less, water to flow through the system. Don't adjust this because if it's turned too low it may leave sprinkler heads at the end of the line without sufficient flow to operate properly. Though smaller, the #2 valve is the "bleeder valve" that can be used to open the valve without using the automatic controller. This valve comes in handy when you are working on the system and must turn valves off and on during maintenance or repair.

Sprinkler and Drip System Maintenance

These checklists will help you to keep your water systems operating at peak efficiency so you'll never waste a drop.

Spray System: Turn on the system manually to ensure each head is working properly. Observe where accumulated minerals from the water may restrict flow or interfere with the delivery pattern. Watch the pop-up heads, which may not be extending as they should. Often grains of sand can become lodged between the housing and the movable core. Watch the gear-driven heads that may jam when particles of sand or soil enter the central rotor. Silt buildup anywhere in the garden can be a clue that a line or fitting is broken or cracked underground. Silt buildup around a head could indicate a broken riser or T-fitting underground.

Drip System: Inspect your emitters often to ensure they are flowing properly. These little parts are cheap, so if there is any chance of malfunction, replace the emitter immediately. Follow each supply line from the valve to the last head and inspect for signs of moisture (which will indicate unusual seepage). In very hot, dry climates or very cold ones, the lifespan of plastic is shorter and becomes brittle sooner. Seepage from cracks can alter the system-wide pressure that will reduce water to plants at the ends. The flush plug or end clamp at the far end of each line allows you to flush the system of any debris, algae, bugs, or minerals that may build up inside to potentially clog emitters. Simply remove the flush plug, open the valve to let it flow freely for a few seconds, then replace.

This traditional rain barrel catches rain by an open-top half barrel, which also allows water to be readily scooped out of the top to pour onto plants, just as the pioneers did.

Micro-Spray System: With a micro-spray system, turn on the system and inspect every head for full water delivery. Often plants grow up in front of them, which will block coverage, so add new heads or move existing ones to restore even coverage. For both types of low-pressure systems, clean out the filter at least once a month. It's located close to the valve or hose bib that supplies the water. In areas where water mineral content is high, the filter can fill up quickly and restrict flow, compromising the efficiency of the system.

Guerilla Water Harvesting

Gardeners overcome their water challenges with creative solutions. Some are truly new solutions and some are rediscoveries from similar challenges faced by our ancestors.

Long before the availability of sprinkler systems and pressurized water, farm wives were forced to water their gardens with well water. But if that was in short supply, they resorted to rain barrels. Rain barrels would catch the water draining from the roof and store it for future use. With our new emphasis on water conservation, the rain barrel is making a comeback with modern designs that easily attach to downspouts from gutter systems. The new rain barrels are fitted with an easy-to-use spigot system that eliminates the need to ladle or siphon out water as they did in the old days.

The use of gray water is another old idea that's being resurrected. Before rural homes had septic systems, homeowners piped used house water ("gray water") to pastures and orchards. Many a nineteenth-century farmhouse garden was supported by gray water as a year-round source of irrigation water. As communities became less agrarian and homes were located closer together, problems arose from excess concentrated gray water,

This modern version of the old-fashioned rain barrel includes a spigot to make the water easier to tap. Plus the new rain barrels are designed so that the top of the barrel is closed, keeping the contents clean and debris free.

which can become a health hazard if it's not properly managed. It is particularly problematic if water tainted by dangerous bacteria from kitchens or bathrooms is drained this way. This is why gray water use is banned in many residential areas.

As we reconsider old ideas for new water conservation practices, gray water remains controversial, but it can be a real lifesaver in arid regions of the West or where extreme drought threatens the survival of a home garden. However, while its use is discussed, breaking the law is not condoned. Check your local ordinances.

The simplest way to experiment with gray water harvesting is to utilize water from the washing machine. It features an easy-access drain that can sometimes be piped through a wall or under the floor to the outside garden. Although washing machine water is ideal for ornamental areas, it should not be used in the food garden.

One example of gray water usage is illustrated by the ingenuity of a California woman. She lived in a rural area where her septic system was barely able to accommodate her household needs and her well was a poor producer. Whenever she did laundry the system backed up into the house. Since she didn't have the money to redo the septic nor drill another well, she put together a simple laundry gray water system. It bypassed the house drainage and augmented her meager water supply. She utilized a roll of two-inch-diameter flexible black pipe and duct-taped it to the washer drainpipe. It ran out to her antique roses that lined the edge of an extensive wood deck. Then she carved a channel under the deck so that the water could flow to each of the rose bushes. Later she utilized a larger diameter perforated pipe that distributed water more efficiently to the foundation planting of roses. The system worked exceptionally well because she used baking soda laundry detergent that lacked dyes and perfumes. The roses grew into enormous sizes, not only due to the consistent water but because the soap contained nitrogen and phosphorous, two common components in fertilizer. Each time they were watered they were fed, too. There wasn't a problem with accumulations of soap or minerals because the annual rains washed it all away. Fresh rainwater also leached through the soil surface so the soap and minerals were not overly concentrated there. Her garden proved that necessity is indeed the mother of invention, and the roses plus their nutritious hip fruits in fall offered beauty, fragrance, and natural medicine in the form of the hips. There is no better way to budget garden than this.

This native Washingtonia filifera was so valuable, providing early Native Americans with wood, shelter, food, and tools in an otherwise barren land.

Palms: 2-for-1 Water Conservative Plants with Many Features

The palm has always been a sign of water in the desert and few plants are as valuable in drought-stricken regions. Palms that hail from desert ecosystems such as those of North Africa, the Canary Islands, Mexico, and California can be surprisingly cold hardy, too. The palm is the signature style maker for gardens that feature an exotic Moroccan style or lush tropical look, but they also do well amidst Mediterranean-inspired architecture.

The famous Phoenix dactylifera was essential in the Middle East and North Africa where its fruit, the date, was a delicacy. The fronds offered thatch, and its spreading umbrella canopy offered shade in courtyards, squares, and mosques.

But the palm is far more valuable than its aesthetic or shade-giving value. It can produce raw materials that are useful in many ways—and free! For example, those palms with fan-shaped fronds are the source of valuable fiber that can be torn into thin strips to tie around a gift wrapped in recycled paper bags. Weaving the palm fronds into decorative crosses and flowers is an old-time craft that originated to preserve Palm Sunday sprigs. The history and directions on how to weave the fibers can be found online at many different sites searched under the keywords "palm + weaving." Palm fronds can also be wired to a sparse overhead arbor to give it seasonal shade or to lend a more tropical look. The frond stems known as petioles can be cut and woven into a rustic picket fence. Those palms that bear fruit can be the source of thousands of easy-to-grow seedlings you can sell. If you live in a good palm-growing region you may find some rare old specimens around town. Keep an eye on them for seed production because there can be a real demand for blue leaf types or other oddballs. Gather the seed, identify the parent, and put your seeds on eBay to sell for extra cash. (It's important to harvest seeds in a legal and neighborly fashion and *never* take *anything* from federal or state parks.)

Common Palms for Home Planting That Tolerate Some Winter Cold

Botanical Name	Common Name	Characteristics	Cold Hardiness
Chamerops humilis	Mediterranean Fan Palm	10 feet tall, multiple trunked, very slow growing	Hardy to 0° F
Phoenix canariensis	Canary Island Date Palm	Enormous tree, single trunk, long feather-shaped fronds	Modestly cold hardy to low 20s
Sabal palmetto	Cabbage Palm	60 feet tall, single trunk	Hardy to 0°F
Trachycarpus fortunei	Windmill Palm	10–20 feet tall, single trunk, slow growing	Hardy to 10°F
Washingtonia filifera	California Fan Palm	40 feet tall, single trunk, fast growing, seed	Hardy to low 20s

6 Don't Throw It Away:
Recycle and reuse everything.

Use it up, wear it out, make it do, or do without.
— New England Proverb

During the early 1970s back-to-the-land movement, hippies headed to rural areas and wilderness to create unconventional homesteads and farms. They wanted to get away from a materialistic world to focus on the basics of living, with less dependence on consumerism. Today's approach is the same, but different: instead of going elsewhere to live more frugally, we are reinventing ideas for use in the everyday household. You can stay right where you are to achieve a real degree of independence.

Homestead is a word that implies a self-contained place where a family lived with minimal help from the outside world. Today the word "homestead" involves rediscovered ideas from early America and the agrarian revolution of the 1970s, but is altered somewhat to fit modern lifestyles, opportunities, and limitations. These alterations include reusing and repurposing what you'd otherwise throw away, such as recycling our waste into useful compost. And most of all, it involves turning our yard into a productive place where every plant has multiple roles.

A great example of this planting adaptation is the hard pruning of willows to promote useful straight growth that can be harvested each year for stakes and fencing; this makes as much sense today as in the past. And just as every farmstead had its "boneyard" of discarded items that was used for

Each year this farmer trims his great old willow trees to harvest the branches, which grow straight and true in a single season. He will select the best ones for reusing on the farm in a variety of ways.

repairs and replacements, today's disposables are waiting to be assessed to determine if they can find new life in the garden.

This chapter is all about the mindset and lifestyle of the budget gardener and the potential for everyone to

This delightful bench, which was made entirely from a recently felled birch tree, offers a beautiful focal point that didn't cost a penny.

This recreation of a medieval peasant's dooryard illustrates how green willow was used to create the first picket-style fences. Note the archway over the gate, which was simply created from larger green branches that were stuck into the soil where they rooted; now the arch itself is a living thing.

have a productive urban homestead. The key is to help you shift from a consumer mentality to one of a hunter-gatherer. The costs of gardening rose at least in part because of our lust for convenience. For example, rather than propagating our own plants, we bought *everything*. But with a bit of creativity coupled with some elbow grease, we can garden even better than before for a fraction of the price using the age-old tricks of the American homesteader.

Wood

Sticks—Never Throw Them Out Again

Visit less-developed countries and you learn very quickly how important sticks are. They are woven into walls for daub-and-wattle houses. They are strung together for fencing. Branches are carved into chairs. They are used for stakes, walking sticks, and shade arbors. And what's left after that becomes fuel. There is no end to the way human ingenuity can utilize these byproducts of trees and shrubs.

All over America, urban waste management departments pick up prunings at curbside. Some folks carefully bundle up these prunings to make them easier to take away. Perhaps they'll be fed into a chipper and then eventually dumped into a compost heap. But for people who are creative and out early in the morning, these sticks can be gleaned for free to save a lot of money in the garden.

Whenever you prune, or when you have a tree or shrub removed from the landscape, you will be left with waste material. Long, whiplike growths, usually suckers from around the base of a tree, are the most useful. These grow quickly, are very straight and evenly tapered, and usually lack side branches. If you think about how you might use the material as you're pruning, you can cut them down to size as you go, eliminating work later. You'll develop an eye for the right kind of material, and once trimmed they can be set aside to harden off (cure).

If you don't have material to harvest in your own yard, begin "garbage day harvesting." The night before pick-up is the best time to hunt for good materials that might be turned into a fine fence or arbor. Your efforts will be most rewarded during winter or early spring, which is the season for pruning dormant plants.

If you have an ambitious project in mind, material in much larger quantities can be obtained from orchard farmers. Similarly, if largescale tree trimming is being done in your neighborhood, this can be a bonanza. These days, with landfill dumping prices so high, many trimmers and gardeners are more than happy for you to relieve them of a part of their dumping cost.

Calling Sticks by Name

Twig: A twig is a rigid kind of stick often from slow-growing trees such as oaks.

Whip: Whips are the fast-growing flexible growth that is either unique to certain species or develops as a sucker or water sprout.

Cane: The segmented rods of bamboo or other grass-like species are called cane.

Pole: Poles are large-diameter straight wood from large suckering trees such as poplar or naturally narrow ones such as lodgepole pine. Native Americans used poles to support their tepees.

Coppicing–An Endless Supply of Sticks

This photo shows the way green willow was used to bind picket fences in the past when iron nails were a valuable commodity both in Europe and colonial America.

On early American homesteads, nails were expensive and always in short supply. This created a demand for flexible materials to bind split-rail fences and for straight twigs to make frontier picket fences to keep critters out of the garden. Long strands of weeping willow were favored for split-rail bindings because they were easy to wrap when green and when they dried in this contorted shape they bound the fence securely.

Poplar and willow are two of the fastest-growing trees, and their tendency to produce quality suckers in quantity made them an important resource. A farmer would start a few of these trees on his land if there were no comparable wild plants available. Each winter the trees would be cut back severely to the stumps, stimulating vigorous suckering during the following growing season, every other year or so. Many Native American tribes practiced coppicing of wild plants to encourage production of certain growth suited to basket making. But since poplar and willow are so vigorous and invasively rooting, and because coppicing does not render them particularly attractive, this method is recommended only for larger homesites where coppiced plants can be hidden from view.

On a larger scale, this concept is used to produce poles in countries where timber is scarce. Plantations and tree farms in drier climates cannot support water-hungry species such as poplar or willow, so the trees used are the highly drought-tolerant eucalyptus and acacia, which sprout readily from stumps. They are planted in closely spaced rows like an orchard, and after the first harvest the stumps are allowed to sucker. Fire and pruning are used to eliminate any lateral growth in order to produce the longest, most evenly tapered poles possible. Anyone who lives on a large homesite with the space to produce such poles will find they have dozens of uses, from fence posts to roof joists, which cost no more than the price of gas to fuel the chainsaw.

These corkscrew willow branches from coppiced trees produce a valuable crop of wavy poles.

Chop Sticks–Recycling Bamboo and Cane

Bamboo is among the most sustainable of all materials. It has literally supplied Asia with everything from kitchen implements to paper and building materials for eons. Bamboo is a goldmine for budget gardeners because cane makes the strongest and most attractive sticks. Each new bamboo sprout from the root is called a *clum*. The clums have no lateral branching to disturb bamboo's straight, gradually tapering forms, which are strong and resist decomposition.

Corkscrew Willow: A 2-for-1 Plant

It is hard to believe that this unique shade tree is a willow, and when you get a close look at the dormant branches, it is more like a sculpture! When you plant the corkscrew willow as a shade tree you get a bonus of all the twisted sticks you can handle. The species is *Salix matsudana* 'Tortuosa', which may be easily rooted from cuttings. In fact, if you buy one "mother" tree, you can use it to make cuttings to root many more. Bundles of leafless corkscrew willows sell for many dollars at craft stores, and you can sell your excess, too. After pruning or thinning in winter when it's bare, you can take your pick of the twisted sticks, which will range from six inches to sixteen feet or more in length. To prevent buds from sprouting leaves in the sudden warmth of your home, lay them on a flat surface to dry outdoors before you sell them or use them indoors.

In the old South, every farmer planted a cane break on the property. Not only was this an age-old source of fishing poles, they also helped poor rural farmers the same ways they serve a modern budget gardener who needs them for staking, trellises, and fences. For an urban homestead, a small cane break is equally valuable, and with continual harvesting these fast-spreading plants are less likely to take over.

Cane is technically a grass with very rigid stems called clums, each divided into individual segments. Each tightly compressed clum develops underground; then, once it grows, these expand

The Japanese have made bamboo fence building an art. They lash the canes together into all sorts of shapes and patterns.

or telescope higher and higher until they reach full size. Many bamboo species grown in gardens produce clums that begin as very soft tissue and may be cut from the ground to yield delicious bamboo shoots, a delicacy in Asian cuisine.

Green Choices

Harvest Bamboo To Protect Native Plants

In many parts of America bamboo has become a rampant weed quite capable of engulfing entire homesites. In the South, bamboo can easily invade wild areas to displace vital native species. You can help control these unwanted exotics while supplying all the bamboo canes you need by harvesting from these problem stands. Be sure to inquire with the property owner before harvesting these free resources.

To grow your own bamboo, keep in mind that there are two groups based on their growth habits. Running bamboos, like runner grasses, are fast growing and aggressive with well-deserved bad reputations. Clumping bamboos tend to be far more well

behaved, and though they will "travel," they prefer to walk, making them more manageable. While you may think that growing bamboo is just for people who live in the tropics, think again. There are many cold-hardy species from the mountains of Asia that can grow farther north than you imagine. Bamboo species can range in size from delicate black stem bamboo that's quite decorative to enormous timber species that produce huge canes suitable for building structures.

Large timber bamboo species can provide an endless supply of good-sized poles that can be utilized to create fences, shade arbors, tree stakes, and decorative rods. Though it may appear tropical, there are many cold-hardy bamboos suited to more temperate climates.

With all these factors—habit, size, and cold hardiness—it pays to do your research before you buy. Check out these excellent Internet sites to find out more about bamboos and to buy them online. Few local garden centers carry them because they quickly outgrow their containers.

Bamboo Garden http://www.bamboogarden.com

Bamboo Inspiration http://www.bamboo-inspiration.com

J M Bamboo Nursery http://www.jmbamboo.com

Stick Preparation and Storage

It is important to know how to prepare sticks for use. For most practical purposes gardeners want sticks that are straight and strong to make pole bean teepees, fences, or dahlia stakes. But creative gardeners may also want to bend their sticks to create furniture, arches over gateways, and binding for paling fences. Here's how to prepare both types:

Experts who make bent willow furniture often cut the willow in early spring, just when the sap begins to flow and the buds swell. But for most other uses you can cut year-round, and if the material must bend or be flexible enough to weave, it must be used immediately. To bend sticks that are too stiff, soak them in water to maintain their softness for a limited time. Another approach is to wrap new cuttings in wet carpet to retain the moisture as they are used. Otherwise, every day after being cut a stick dries, growing stiffer and stiffer. Bending willow is a great start for topiary forms

Smaller bamboo species, such as this Phyllostachys aurea, *are the best choice for producing small diameter stakes for perennials and annuals. These bamboos can be rather invasive, however, so to control spread, plant them in the ground inside a 15-gallon nursery container.*

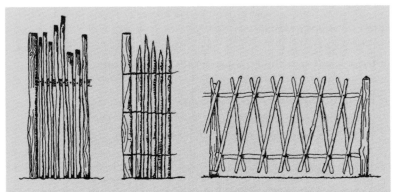

Left: *This is similar to the first picket fences of Plymouth Colony. Split stakes were pounded into the soil and the tops were connected by a stringer.* **Center:** *Another adaptation of the picket fence uses intact sticks that have been sharpened to a point. The sticks are then woven together with twisted wire stringers.* **Right:** *This is just one of many adaptations of sticks transformed into rigid decorative fences.*

or small shapes that may be used in container gardens to hold lightweight annual vines or dwarf ivies.

If the cuttings are to be used as stakes or supports of any kind, they should be allowed to dry on a clean, flat surface. A concrete slab or pea gravel field are fine for drying, or you can even put them on a roof. If the cutting sags or bends even slightly, the dried twig will retain that curve. In most climates, the sticks should be dried in the sun to avoid rotting as they harden off. Once dried, store the stakes under cover on a solid surface where they are no longer exposed to sun or moisture that can shorten their lifespan. If the sticks are free of rot or termites, these poles and whips can be used for many years to come.

Tightwad Gardening Tip

Even thorny twigs of roses, ocotillo, and berry vines can be useful. Use small segments carefully arranged in pots and planters to keep cats and dogs from spoiling house-plants and flowers.

Stick Fencing

In woodcuts of medieval Europe, the first gardens were enclosed by wattle fences. These are woven just like a flat basket panel using willows coppiced along the riverbeds. Wattle fencing was important for wind control as well and created warm pockets for winter gardens where there was little opportunity for fresh food. The same idea was used to create walls smeared with mud in daub-and-wattle construction, common in those days.

Wattle utilizes a series of vertical stays or tightly spaced posts secured into the soil. Green wood whips are then woven horizontally in and out of the posts until they provide a completely opaque wall. Once the woven wood dries, the fence hardens to become very durable and stable. Building a wattle fence from scratch is a difficult but rewarding way to create a naturalistic garden barrier.

When the pilgrims came to the New World, they protected their gardens from livestock and wildlife with paling fences. This rustic ancestor of the picket fence was made from twigs or split stakes pounded into the ground at close intervals. A single top rail was lashed across the tops to hold them together; later the top rail was connected by nails or wire. This type of fence appears worldwide, made of as many different kinds of wood or cane as there are trees. This type of fence is easier to build if you use sticks of similar diameter that have been dried flat until they are rigid enough to stand up well. The top need not be even, as the irregular lengths add character.

This traditional wattle fence of medieval gardens shows how beautifully it can suit a unique garden setting. Beside it is the tree from which the twigs came; the tree will be "beheaded" whenever its new straight top growth reaches the desired diameter for the twigs.

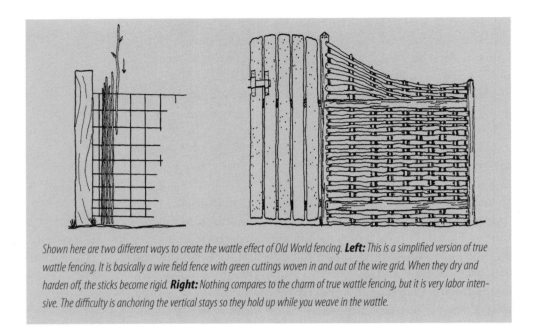

*Shown here are two different ways to create the wattle effect of Old World fencing. **Left:** This is a simplified version of true wattle fencing. It is basically a wire field fence with green cuttings woven in and out of the wire grid. When they dry and harden off, the sticks become rigid. **Right:** Nothing compares to the charm of true wattle fencing, but it is very labor intensive. The difficulty is anchoring the vertical stays so they hold up while you weave in the wattle.*

Cane and bamboo have raised fence design to an art form in Japan. The cane is drilled with small holes into which wire is threaded to secure the fastenings. Those who have the skill and ability for such projects should explore traditional Japanese fencing styles to copy. Otherwise, cane may be used the same way picket fences are, making lovely additions to Asian-inspired gardens.

Farmers in the redwood country of California's north coast created sheep fencing with easy-to-split heartwood. It's still intact a century later.

Garden Uses for Sticks

There are endless uses for twigs in the garden, and anyone with an empty wallet or creative flair will find them indispensable. Once you have a good supply of poles, whips, and canes on hand, you'll discover new ways to use them in your garden.

Plant and Flower Stakes

Straight twigs make beautiful flower stakes. Rather than artificial-looking metal or green painted bamboo, twigs are naturally colored and irregular enough to be quite charming. Swanky orchid growers have begun using twigs to support the delicate flower spires. Larger stakes come in handy in the kitchen garden as well, to support leaning plants burdened by heavy crops. Shorter twigs mark where underground roots or bulbs are in fall planting so they are not accidentally dug up during spring planting.

A Tepee Trellis

If you could take a peek into any Early American kitchen garden, you'd find pole tepees cloaked in bean vines. Simple to make by binding the ends of sticks together with tie wire, tepee trellises may be reused year after year for beans, peas, gourds, and even grapes. Don't disassemble the tepee at the end of the season; just pull it out of the ground, gather the poles together like the spokes of an umbrella, and store it in a dry place for next year.

To discourage intruders or perching birds, farmers often sharpened the tips of their pole fences, which later evolved into the traditional Victorian style of white picket fences.

A Pea Trellis

Peas climb by means of slender tendrils, which wrap more easily around thin objects than thicker ones. That's why garden centers sell special netting both for edible peas and flowering sweet peas. Rather than spend money on such a trellis for climbing peas, save some of your thinnest twiggy branches from winter pruning. First, string a horizontal wire between posts where the peas are to grow. Then, take the branches, turn them upside down, and hang them in this position on the wire so the twig

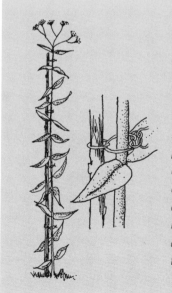

Tall flowers frequently need support stakes to keep them upright. The most natural are the hardened-off prunings of straight but thin limbs. During everyday pruning, separate all the appropriate-sized material and give it time to dry on a clean, flat surface. Don't use the limbs while they are still green because they will be too flexible.

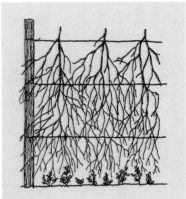

An old-style pea trellis is easy to make using some of your more finer-branched winter prunings. These twiggy branches are attached upside down to a wire stringer so that the finest twigs at the tips are within reach of the developing pea vines.

tips nearly touch the ground. These slender tips are ideal for young pea tendrils to grab hold and are stronger farther up for when the vines mature and need better support.

A Wall Trellis

Nothing is more charming than a decorative wall trellis made of twigs and branches. Whips with diameters the size of your finger can be lashed with wire or rope into lovely grids and arches. When attached to walls, fences, and doorways, these support climbing plants. Many catalogs sell rustic trellises at high prices, but you can make one just as nice for almost no cost at all—if you've been saving your prunings properly!

There are different ways to attach the joints. Some people prefer to drill holes and make the connections with wood screws, then cover the screw heads with more decorative lashing material such as twine, leather, or green vine runners. Don't forget that any design you choose that requires bends or arches should use green flexible whips so they can be shaped to dry in the proper form.

*Long, straight limbs are ideal for creating a tepee trellis used for climbing bean supports, a method practiced by the early American colonists. **Left:** This is a traditional tepee, which may have many more poles than the few shown here. **Right:** A wider A-frame design allows you to attach wire or netting for more dainty climbing plants such as peas.*

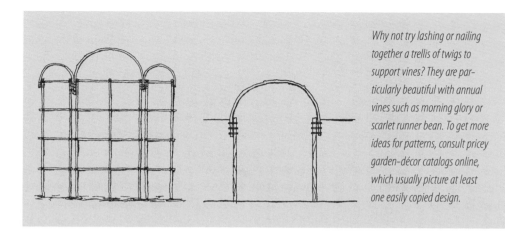

Why not try lashing or nailing together a trellis of twigs to support vines? They are particularly beautiful with annual vines such as morning glory or scarlet runner bean. To get more ideas for patterns, consult pricey garden-décor catalogs online, which usually picture at least one easily copied design.

Step Risers

In many gardens a steeply sloped pathway can become too difficult to use in wet weather. A simple solution is to create widely spaced steps to take up the grade more comfortably. These steps are usually created out of railroad ties placed across the pathway and anchored into place by reinforcing bar or steel pipe pounded into the ground. The area behind the step riser is filled with earth or brick. But you must buy railroad ties, and they are so thick they can be difficult to cut to fit in your location.

The budget gardener might use leftover firewood logs instead. If you have some heavy limbs or cut down a tree, the larger-diameter branches or logs can be employed as step risers, too. These are the free alternatives to landscape timbers. These logs are anchored just like railroad ties. To make the steps safe, use lengths as wide as the path and from six to eight inches in diameter to equal your area's building code riser height.

This pathway utilizes rounded branches for step risers and buried railroad ties for a solid surface to gradually adjust the grade at this gateway.

These willows were cuttings simply stuck into the soil where they have rooted and now produce leaves. You can do the same to create a living arch, arbor, or even a dome-shaped playhouse. The key is to cut dormant willow twigs in winter and insert them deeply into the soil so there is plenty below the ground to sprout a root system.

Gateway Arches

Gateways become something special if they have overhead arches upon which vines or roses can be trained. Whether arched, pointed, or simply flat topped, they transform sticks into quaint architectural features. When enveloped in flowering vines they make especially inviting entries composed of prunings you'd otherwise throw away.

There are many ways to create these arches, depending on the kind of gate you have already in place. What all share are two strong, upright support poles that are attached to the existing gate posts with wood screws, nails, or tie wire. These will carry the weight of the vine and should be securely fastened.

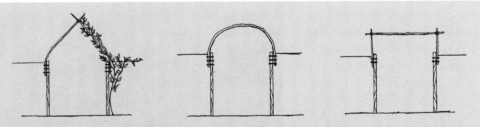

You don't have to hire a carpenter to add those charming vine-shrouded gateways to your house. Simply use the fence posts already in place and attach some stout twigs with wood screws or nails. Then use one of these three design ideas to create an overhead connection. These are just a few of many options you can try, including bundling smaller-diameter twigs to create a thicker arch. Remember, since they are made of unwanted twigs, there's no cost for experimentation.

You can add an arch or crosspiece by using screws or a secure lashing with wire. Exactly how they are placed depends on your design. Always remember that this little structure will take a beating, so when in doubt, choose the most long-lasting connection, such as long wood screws. It helps to pre-drill the holes since dried wood tends to be hard and sometimes brittle and may split under too much pressure.

Shade Arbors or Ramadas

All over the Southwest you'll find twig arbors known as "ramadas" that offer shady outdoor work places. The shade comes from brush and branches laid across the top of a basic structure.

Constructing an arbor is a bigger job, but a whole industry has grown up around the use of treated lodgepole pines as rustic arbors. Anything you cut or find for this use is valuable, since the alternative, milled lumber or lodgepole, can be very expensive. Some of the best sources of pole wood such as acacia, cedar, eucalyptus, maple, and poplar are grown on third-world plantations. The building of heavy overhead structures is a job best left to those experienced in construction to ensure that it will never collapse and cause injury.

In the West, shade structures known as ramadas provided an open-air shaded place to work and gather in comfort. Ramadas in areas where timber was scarce used any kind of twig locally available. This example features long ocotillo twigs closely spaced to create shade.

If rocks are available on your property, by all means use them every way you can instead of buying new materials. Here a simple step face of carefully placed stones creates a series of long, natural-looking steps down this slope.

Fieldstone cobbles are among the least expensive and most common stones there are. In this photo, they are used to face a wine cellar.

What makes a dry stonewall so clever is that lack of mortar allows you to grow plants through the gaps between stones. Roots remain anchored in the soil, which keeps them moist in hot weather.

A Rocky Harvest

For those who must live with the difficulties of rocky soil, there are considerable benefits as well. Some of the most beautiful handmade gardens are composed of pavements, walls, curbs, and rock gardens made with stone dug from the soil on site. The rocky homesite illustrates one of the important principles of budget gardening: always use available materials before buying complicated and expensive alternatives. So if you have rocks, use them!

When you build a raised planter or wall with stones, you'll never have to worry about its decomposition as you do with wood. Stones encrusted with dirt can be cleaned up nicely either by rainfall or sprinklers, even after they've been put to use. Working with stones isn't difficult, but it does take time to gather and transport rocks to the location of your project. You must fit them together as tightly as possible in order to ensure stability. The larger stones must be used at the bottom and the smaller stones placed on top as you build up. For durable, dry stonewalls of any height, the base must be much wider than the top to achieve structural integrity.

Green Choices

One of the biggest causes of wasted resources is when homeowners try to create one kind of garden into a site where it
doesn't belong. This can require excess water, resources, and
building materials, not to mention many dead plants. Living
green means really understanding the nature of your homesite
and working with the opportunities it has to offer as well as using
locally native plants. When you work with Nature rather than
against her, the result is always rewarding.

Rocks of any size are perfect to create a rock garden, one of
the most interesting and charming natural planting schemes. Rock
gardens have long been a solution to very heavy soils that don't
drain. A rock garden is created by placing large stones within the
planting area, then filling between them with soil so the plants are
set well above the surrounding grade. Rock gardens are also created on slopes where fewer rocks are needed and the soil is naturally shallow. The traditional English rock garden was situated on a
south-facing exposure for growing alpine plants that are native to
thin, porous, high-altitude soils. The same conditions make a rock
garden the perfect place both for tropical and cold-hardy succulents that abhor excess water in their root zones.

The beauty of rock gardens is that no two are alike. This is
because the availability and type of stone varies with every region,
and stone in general is not consistent in size, shape, color, or
texture. Many believe the success of rock gardens is because the
stones act as insulation to trap moisture beneath them, which
keeps plant roots cool even when temperatures on the surface
are very high. In the mountains it's not uncommon to see lush
perennial wildflowers sprouting out of barren fractured stone cliffs,
which is a natural example of this same moisture-holding ability.

Top: Use those unwanted rocks and boulders to create a rock garden. Arrange them in a creative pattern, then fill in the gaps with topsoil. When you plant in the pockets, soon nothing
but the stones and flowering plants will be visible. This is an ideal gardening solution for gardens where the soils are very dense or so rocky that normal cultivation is
difficult. *Bottom:* Rocks can be stacked to create raised planter walls. If sufficiently
sized pockets and gaps are allowed, then plants can spill down the wall as well as
grow out the top.

Rock Mulch

A rock mulch uses excess rocks (yours or someone else's) to control weeds and reduce soil moisture loss. Mulch of locally free rocks of any size can be laid directly onto garden soil in a packed single layer. Some weeds do pop through, but not many, particularly if you don't water that area. It's a great way to make a fallow part of your yard look good without plants or cost. Simply be sure you place the rocks as close together as possible. The famous British gardener Vita Sackville-West was quite outspoken about the value of rocks for perennials. She observed that many of her plants growing beside rocks, much as they do in nature, grew more lush and bloomed better. Her conclusion: rocks reduce surface moisture evaporation, thus keeping roots cooler and more evenly moist, particularly in unusually warm weather.

Cobblestone Paving

Until recently, many European lanes were made of cobblestone paving, which is simply rounded river stones set very tightly on a level layer of sand. An excess supply of cobblestones allows gardeners to create similar uneven rustic paving. While that may not be great for stiletto heels, it's just fine for bare feet or shoes. Simply dig out the area of the path to the average depth of your stones less about an inch; then set them into place. Scatter dry concrete into the gaps and water it in. The concrete sets up and you'll have a truly romantic pathway that keeps your feet out of the mud and makes an exceptional feature to surround with beautiful plants.

This simple bank became an alpine rock garden when it was strewn with surplus rocks dug out of a nearby vegetable garden (below left). In the arid West, this rock garden features boulders and a mulch of smaller stones that keep weeds down and fill spaces between geometrically interesting succulents and drought-resistant perennials (below right).

Mixing device: Keep a few milk or juice containers on hand all the time. Fully intact gallon milk jugs are handy when it comes to mixing fertilizers or other water-based products. A gallon container holds exactly one gallon and any leftover contents can be sealed and stored for future use.

Other Reusables

Recycle an old laundry basket into a planter. Repair any cracks with duct tape, then punch holes in the bottom. Line the inside with a garbage bag and poke holes in this as well. Fill the bag with potting soil and enjoy at least one season's worth of leaf or root crops.

Reuse styrofoam food containers and coffee cups for seedling containers. Rinse them out and then just punch a few holes in the bottom and use for a season.

Tightwad Gardening Tip

Save twist ties from products bagged in plastic. They make great connectors for vines and climbing plants. Since plastic garbage bags are always packed with additional ties, allow them to accumulate in the kitchen so there are always plenty of plant ties at your fingertips.

Metals

Throughout Latin America you can find extensive patio and balcony gardens of plants potted in old tins, coffee cans, and other metal containers. Sure, some folks don't like the look once rust sets in, but the budget gardener knows that it's the plant that matters most. It's better to grow plants than to be fussy about what the pot looks like.

Americans throw out millions of tin cans every day, but in third-world countries they are valuable planting pots. This example from Mexico utilizes a canned milk container and the plants are topped off with a mulch of crushed pine needles.

Most of the time we don't pay much attention to containers when shopping, but a budget gardener always keeps an eye out for metal containers. Not only are they great for growing plants but small tins such as Altoid mint containers are excellent for seed storage. Another good example is the beautiful Italian olive oil tins. Since you are buying bottled oil, why not buy in bulk and pick up a great looking plant container, too!

There are also good opportunities for using cans in more unique ways. A big 32-ounce can with the top and bottom cut out yields a clean, smooth cylinder perfect for protecting seedlings from crawling insects. To keep the crawlers from going over the top, smear the edge with molasses so they get bogged down on the outside.

Cylinders also make superior plant protectors for hot, windy locales. They shade the root zone and protect the plant from wind pressure. You can even top it with clear food wrap held by a rubber band to create a mini-greenhouse if there's an unexpected cold snap. Large can cylinders make very good protectors for the base of a young tree or shrub that's vulnerable to string trimmer damage. Simply slice the side of the can open to slide the trunk in, then duct tape if necessary. Go ahead and paint the can the color of the trunk to make it blend in.

Tightwad Gardening Tip

Some households don't generate enough disposables to fill all your garden needs. Your local school can be a gold mine of heavy-duty plastic jugs, restaurant-size cans, and glass jars with screw-top lids. You'll also find millions of single serving milk cartons, yogurt cups, and many types of other paper or plastic reusables.

Because aluminum soda cans don't rust, they retain their bright coloring and make cute little decorative pots or gifts that won't cost a penny.

The tops and bottoms of the cans are also useful, particularly the kind that frozen juices come in, as these don't have ragged edges. They are good bird-scares for fruit trees as are foil pie tins. Punch a hole and thread the pie tin with string; then hang it among the ripening fruit. To preserve the shiny finish and discourage rust, dip the pie tin in liquid plastic sealer or paint with clear nail polish. These also make cute plant labels you can hang on your roses and blueberries to recall the specific varieties.

Small tuna or cat food cans have a specialized use, particularly in the South where ant infestations are epic. Simply place each leg of a patio table into an empty can, then fill with water to about an inch deep. If you're concerned about the can rusting, which would stain pavement or floors, use plastic containers or the bottom half of aluminum soda cans instead.

Wire

Baling wire that used to bind hay bales has been replaced by nylon twine. But wire of any kind is very useful in the garden and when a free source is found, use it for these purposes:

- Thread wire through segments of an old garden hose and use to stake trees.
- Stretch wire between poles for a pea-vine trellis.
- Wrap wire tightly to bind the top of a pole tepee for beans and tomatoes.
- Use wire to bind bundles of twigs for stick arbors over a gateway.
- Weave wire in and out of picket fence sticks to bind sections of rustic fencing.
- Use wire to securely bind sticks for a decorative wall trellis.
- Use wire hangers to make "bobby pins" to anchor weed barrier cloth.
- Use wire to hang pots and moss baskets from overhead structures.

Window Screens

While long-stem plants are easy to dry by hanging them upside down in bundles, not all herbs and flowers lend themselves to this. And material that's shed from the stems may be just as valuable once dried. The old way of drying loose stuff, or plants with stems too weak to hang dry, is to dehydrate them on salvaged window screens. These screens can be covered with plant parts and hung in the garage for a very quick drying solution.

Refrigerator Racks

You can hang dangling bundles of plants by recycling old refrigerator racks. Rather than hanging plants from high rafter nails, suspend metal grills at a height you can easily reach without a ladder. Then tie your bundles with a little wire hook on one end that makes it as easy to put the bundles up to dry as it is to take them down. This is a valuable tip if you do a lot of plant drying in summer.

This beautiful paving was created using cast-off wine bottles. However, a problem with wine bottles is the recessed bottom, which tends to fill with litter and water.

Blue glass mineral water bottles are used here to emphasize the line of the curved paving edge by their perfect spacing.

Glass

Glass is one of the most valuable inexpensive or free materials for gardens. Innovative gardeners and avid wine drinkers have been creating bottle paving for years for a unique look. The bottles are arranged neck side down and pounded into the soil edge to edge. They can also be set into a bed of sand as well. This technique makes beautiful edging as well, particularly if the bottles are cobalt blue or green.

In old Western towns such as Rhyolite, Nevada, you can find houses whose entire walls were made out of bottles. At one time Western boomtowns were packed with saloons, which used thousands of bottles of whiskey. Because building materials were often scarce, bottles were stacked like bricks and mortar to create thick, strong, well-insulated walls that allowed light to pass through. Such an idea would make a beautiful low wall in the garden or patio for nearly no cost.

Other Stuff

Nylons and panty hose: The beauty of cast-off women's hosiery is that they are soft and stretchy yet quite strong. Pantyhose legs make excellent tree or shrub ties, particularly in windy areas where movement from traditional stakes can cause abrasion on a plant's bark. Put a rock in a panty hose toe and tie the leg to a weeping cherry branch to weight it into proper position. Use this trick to encourage other plants to grow downward with the power of gravity.

Mylar balloons: Rather than tossing these non-decomposers, cut Mylar balloons into strips to save for summer. When fruit from a tree or berry bush is close to being ripe, tie the Mylar ribbons into the trees or shrubs for free bird scares.

Candle stubs: If a cork isn't handy, wax candle stubs make perfect plugs or corks. They're ideal if you've lost the lid to a bottle or want to plug the drain hole in a garden pot.

Before you throw out or give away old shoes, reconsider them as plant containers. This pair of hiking boots with drainage holes in the soles makes excellent containers for succulents.

Kitchen grease: If you live in cold winter country, save this vital fuel source for birds. The drippings of beef produce thicker fat or tallow when it is cooled so keep this separate from bacon and chicken drippings. Beef tallow remains harder at higher temperatures while other kinds of fat melt. Tallow can be mixed with oats or wild birdseed, then packed into pinecones in lieu of peanut butter. You can also just pack the cone with grease and roll the outside in birdseed.

7 Tips and Tricks:
Twice the garden for half the price.

I'm excited about turning an old, rusted, broken-down wheelbarrow of ours into a garden landscape. I'm also going to try tire planters but when it comes to toilets in my front yard, it's not happening.

—Julie in FL, Frugal Gardening Forum, Get Crafty.com

America is truly the land of plenty and there is much opportunity to garden less expensively or free here. The problem is we've been conditioned to buy what we need instead of scrounging around for free stuff. True ingenuity and a bit of hard work yield what no money can buy because necessity is always the mother of invention.

A rarely discussed aspect of garden design is this: some of the most interesting and innovative landscapes use unorthodox materials and elements. These are some of the true standout gardens with a major *wow* factor. Why? It's because they are genuinely unique. They don't use the same pavers, art, and landscape timbers everyone else uses. They solve problems in unusual ways that often results in a truly groundbreaking look. It's people who are limited by cost who dream the best ideas. And from these gardeners who take risks, who experiment like true artists, we inherit a treasure trove of ideas we'd never have conjured ourselves.

One of the best sources for materials and garden decoration can be found at house demolition yards. With lumber prices skyrocketing, the value of torn-down material is growing all the time. Special companies listed under "Demolition" or "House Demolition" in local Internet directories or the Yellow Pages are hired to tear down and salvage old buildings. In the East where the cities are much older you'll

Demolition salvage yards like this one can be found all across America. They are a budget gardener's treasure trove for all sorts of unusual, often one-of-a-kind items.

find some of the best opportunities for salvage materials. Among these items are copper pipe, Victorian gingerbread trim, windows, doors, cabinets, screens, beams, and plumbing fixtures, as well as all sorts of wood products carefully dismantled and stored at their yard.

Demolition yards also pick up odd lots of surplus building materials such as sliding glass doors and discarded large appliances. The rest of the world may call it a junkyard, but to a budget gardener a demolition yard is full of treasures.

Whether found at a garage sale or at an antique fair, the aged patina on this old, steel garden chair from the 1950s serves both as a one-of-a-kind accent as well as convenient seating.

Wood

Demolition yard wood is great for creating a rustic look or building cold frames. Naturally weathered siding turns a new shed into a focal point or lets it settle into the landscape as though it has been there for decades.

Keep an eye out for special architectural elements such as columns that might have once supported a front porch. A pair can serve as the supports for a stunning gateway, and if you're lucky you might find four to build a pergola. However, columns have grown quite expensive. A better buy would be a damaged old column that might have one good end that you can cut off to make a beautiful pedestal for a birdbath or sundial.

This bare wall became the backdrop for a series of salvaged six-pane windows painted in a bright color making a $10 purchase the focal point of the adjacent garden.

In a good salvage yard you might find sections of old picket fence. These can be quite nice as freestanding artistic elements that need not enclose anything. They also are fine partitions to help physically and visually break up a large garden into smaller "rooms" or nooks. If you can find elaborate old Victorian-style spans, they make truly lovely trellises for rambling morning glories or delicate sweet peas. You can either repaint or use the shabby chic look for a charming patina.

This rustic entry to a country home's driveway was created from sections of wood fence and wrought iron salvaged from an old homesite. Although it merely encloses a pasture, the addition of such unique free materials presents a charming appearance.

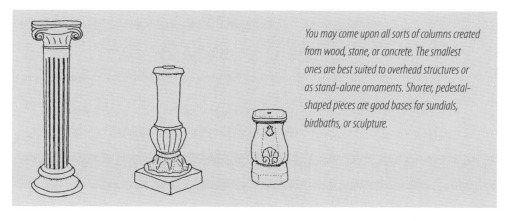

You may come upon all sorts of columns created from wood, stone, or concrete. The smallest ones are best suited to overhead structures or as stand-alone ornaments. Shorter, pedestal-shaped pieces are good bases for sundials, birdbaths, or sculpture.

Finials can be made of wood, stone, or concrete. They can top fence posts, balustrades, or newel posts, or simply stand alone to mark the edges of patios and terraces. Restored finials can grace the top of a gazebo or garden shed.

Fence pickets were created with many different decorative tips; some were simple points and others were highly ornate. Look for sections of fence or single pickets.

Old Door Potting Table

Old solid-core doors, particularly if the surface has a little detail, make fine potting tables or surfaces for creating outdoor garden crafts. Lay a door on a pair of sawhorses to provide plenty of surface for repotting and to store your supplies.

Metal Fencing

Once metal fencing became more affordable during the nineteenth century, almost every homeowner enclosed the front yard. Fences became a public display of success and neighbors strived to find the most ornate designs for their homes. Interestingly, it also became popular to fence gravesites, which led to many smaller sections landing in salvage yards when old cemeteries were moved.

Metal fencing either is cast iron, wrought iron, or woven wire. The first two are rigid, the third, flexible. Cast iron is very heavy, brittle, and subject to rust, so there are more bits and pieces of this kind of thing around than the other types. Cast iron is difficult if not impossible to repair by welding, so it's not easily reused into other structural components. But since iron can be cast into very ornate patterns, these are the most decorative. They can be used as a fence or hung on walls to display the workmanship of antique pieces. Wrought iron is the most versatile because, unlike cast iron, it takes to welding just fine. It can be repaired and changed

Architectural Garden Art To Hunt For

Glass electrical insulators	Weathervane pieces	Ornate thresholds
Cast iron wood stove pieces	Signs	Drawer pulls
Crystal or glass doorknobs	Crystal chandelier pieces	Dresser drawers
Ceramic-coated kitchen stove panels	Wrought iron grill	Zinc plates
	Shutters	Antique washtubs and sinks
Odd finials	Broken pottery or planters	Claw foot tubs
Ceramic faucet handles	Broken fountain parts	

into something useful, such as turning a span on end, attaching some hinges, and turning it into a gate. Twisted wire is a real find, particularly if it's still in fairly good condition. The pattern is simple, arched at the top and denser at the base, but it's ideal for fencing pets out of a veggie garden or keeping children inside their play yard.

Decorative iron fence panels are designed for a horizontal orientation, but if a section is turned on its end, it can become a beautiful gate. Consult a welder to reinforce or add hinges to any fencing you find in a demolition yard if you want to create a gate.

From Ordinary to Extraordinary

If you're planning to build a masonry wall, you can integrate pieces of old iron fencing or ornate heat registers to cover openings that allow you to peer through to the rest of the garden beyond. These openings also facilitate critically important air circulation in smaller urban gardens. In fact, fencing or heat registers combined with stacked bottles, colored tile fragments, and bits of architectural detailing in terracotta or stone can turn an ordinary wall into a one-of-a-kind design statement.

Victorian wood stoves are beautiful as garden art and may be used as a surface for plants or for a single focal point.

Montage of Metal

Keep an eye out for miscellaneous pieces of hardware that can be made of iron, copper, or bronze. Don't buy a new pull for the gate—find an older decorative one. Even if you don't have a lock, the metal plates with the keyholes can be screwed onto a gate to give it the illusion of age. Some salvage yards have hardware mixed up in bins, so take some time to look at each piece. Under the dirt, rust, or corrosion you might find a jewel.

This post is topped with a cast iron leg salvaged from an old appliance and topped with a piece of red glass.

This bottle tree, based on an old southern tradition, features brightly colored bottles that glint in the sunlight.

At the Northwest Garden Show this design illustrates how beautiful vintage tin ceiling panels can be when they're set in the ground and sur-rounded by a densely growing carpet of green.

Appliances and Claw Tubs

Places that accept broken appliances often remove the recyclable materials and then store the rest. Washing machine drums are thicker than dryer drums and they are ideal for gardens because they are studded with holes that ensure good drainage. You can paint over all but the lowest rows of holes to make the drum more solid. These can last forever and make exceptional containers for vegetables and small fruit trees due to their strength and overall size.

Claw foot tubs that are irreparably cracked or stained make wonderful water gardens. Their size and strength ensures they will never rot or disintegrate. Though they are heavy they can be moved if you wish and they are very easy to clean. The outside surface can be painted to blend into a background while lotus or water lilies bloom on the surface. If you want to make an old claw foot tub into a raised planter, be sure the drain hole is open and line the bottom of it with pottery shards or gravel to ensure the entire soil mass drains evenly.

Many older doors and gates were built with oversized decorative hinges. Take the time to see the beauty beneath the rust, and if you come upon any that are bronze, snatch them up.

This painted old wood stove becomes the perfect surface to display a recycled teapot turned mosaic, an antique steam iron, and old Mason jars.

Concrete

Flagstone is one of the most beautiful traditional garden making material, but unfortunately its also the most expensive. This is partly because stone is so heavy to transport and fuel is so costly. But, the lower cost of flagstone at the quarry can be affordable for even the most cash-strapped budget gardener.

It's not difficult to make a planter out of an old washing machine drum. First find a drum and remove the agitator if necessary. Then paint the outside with asphalt driveway sealer but leave the bottom few rows of holes open to ensure drainage. Finish the outside with sticks, planks, mosaics, or any other decorative material you have on hand.

Salvaging broken concrete fragments to use as faux flagstone isn't a new idea in gardens, but if it's done well it can look just fabulous. If the pieces all come from of the same slab that may have a golden or pinkish cast, try to use these exclusively in your pathway or paving to give it a more integrated look. Otherwise you'll have the ordinary gray concrete that may vary considerably from piece to piece. A way to give it a more integrated look is to thin some wood stain and paint it on the concrete. It will stain the surface a more natural color, unifying the walk or patio.

Concrete pieces can also be used to create curbs and low walls. The uniform thickness of concrete allows it to stack well, leaving the broken edges on the outside and the finished surface of the top piece visible. Stacking can be used to create a dry stone wall up to about two feet tall, or a larger step back wall built against a slope. If you build your concrete wall to retain or hold soil, leave small openings between the layers for planting.

Even though this raised bed is composed of broken pavers, concrete fragments are treated exactly the same way.

You can also use small concrete fragments partially buried on their sides to edge flower beds and lawns. The depth to which you bury a fragment depends on the soil conditions, but it must be enough to keep the fragment upright when the earth is wet. You may be running power equipment around the edge of the lawn and these pieces must be stable enough to remain neatly in place.

Concrete isn't the only waste material that can be used in gardens. Broken bricks, pavers, and concrete block are versatile and can create a more varied and interesting effect. Crazy quilt paving, even if it's only in a small area, can be a real bonus to a garden's design. If there's a masonry job going on in your neighborhood, the contractor is likely to give you all his broken pieces if you take them away because that means he won't have to take them to the dump and pay dump fees. Yet another source are masonry supply yards where they often have a great deal of broken pavers and units lying around.

> ## Tightwad Gardening Tip
>
> One of the least known upscale sources of budget paving material can be found at "slab shops" where they cut granite countertops. For each sink or raw end that is cut from the finished counter, there will be a remnant of truly amazing stone. Granite is so strong it rarely breaks and it is already polished, offering endless opportunities to someone with a creative mind.
>
> Tile supply houses are among the most productive sources for creative gardeners, particularly if you enjoy the art of mosaic design or decide to tackle simple tile setting. The various manufacturers are always phasing out one line or another, so these suppliers are often happy to give you their extra samples. If you don't want to set tile the traditional way, you can use simple one-foot-square concrete steppingstones as a base and glue the tiles on. These masonry glues are very strong and weatherproof. Use all the tile samples to create crazy little mosaics to use all over your garden. You'll pay a dollar per steppingstone, about the same in glue, and the salvaged tiles are *free!*

Super Cheap or Free Gardening Ideas
Venetian or Mini-blinds

Whether you're dealing with wood shutters or plastic or metal blinds, they all offer slats of material that you can use a variety of ways in your garden. Slats from mini-blinds are perfectly sized to create weatherproof labels. These slats can be easily cut with scissors or tin snips so that one end is pointed to slide into seed trays effortlessly. Use a permanent marker or a black Sharpie to write the labels. They are perfect for marking shrubs, perennials, and roses in the landscape for long-lasting identification.

Longer segments of the old 2.5-inch-wide metal blinds stand up more stiffly and can be used to divide a flat into sections.

Simply cut them with tin snips to the desired length and push the edge about an inch into the soil. In the garden they can also be used to enclose the edges of creeping plants to keep them more strictly confined.

Burlap Bags

Old or new burlap bags are a perfect way to grow potatoes in the city. Unlike plastic bags, burlap allows plenty of air exchange and drainage. Simply fill a bag up with good soil and plant the seed potatoes on top. An alternative method is to fill the bag with soil, close it securely with wire or rope, then lay it down on its side. Cut small holes down the middle and plant the seed potatoes through these. Put the bags in a sunny location, whether on paving, gravel, or soil, and keep them moist. By the time you're ready for harvest, the burlap will be decomposing and you need only cut it open to gather the spuds. This method of burlap bag agriculture also works well for leaf and root crops.

Cable Spools

Wood cable spools and their more contemporary plastic counterparts will stand up to severe weather. The smaller versions make fine side tables for lawn chairs while the larger wood types may be painted to create a lovely outdoor dining surface. It's not hard to find cable spools if you inquire at the local power company, telephone company, cable TV installer, or electrical contractor.

Never throw away a burlap bag or a sturdy woven fiber feed bag. Instead, use it as a potato planter that is guaranteed to grow great spuds. Other root crops also like growing in this method because of the soft texture of potting soil.

Buckets

Few items are more useful to gardeners than a good stout bucket with a tight-fitting lid. The best ones are those used by food service or to contain swimming pool chlorine, so inquire with those businesses to find free sources. Many equine supplements come in very good-quality buckets with lids that you can pick up at racetracks and stables. Even kitty litter now comes in solid

plastic buckets, and neighbors who own these pets will have
plenty to throw away. Drill a few holes in the bottom and you've
also got a perfect long-lasting vegetable planter.

Treadle Sewing Machine

One of the most charming table bases for outdoor furniture
comes from reusing a treadle sewing machine that was driven
manually by a foot plate. Those that are entirely made out of
steel or wrought iron, particularly when they are ornate Victorian
designs, are best.

Inner Tubes

Large-sized small-diameter inner tubes like those for 10-speed
racing bikes make excellent ties to secure trees to a support
stake. They stretch and bend with the wind, reducing abrasion
on the trunk. Inner tubes can be sliced to create giant rubber
bands or long strips for tying shrubs and other smaller plants.

*Ordinary galvanized
metal buckets as
well as garbage
cans make fine
containers for
plants. These have
holes drilled in the
bottom for drainage
and offer a perfect
home for hostas.*

Old Red Wagons

No matter how dented and rusted, those old red wagons we all knew as youngsters make great helpers in the garden. Their narrow wheelbase and tight turning radius are ideal for small city gardens too cramped for traditional wheelbarrows.

Cloth Nail Apron

When you're out pruning plants or performing any of the many tasks from sowing seed to mending fences, cloth nail aprons put tools and supplies at your fingertips. Watch for hardware store promotions to get a free one. Compare them with official "gardener's tool belts" and you'll realize this is a true budget gardener find.

Wire Coat Hangers

While we aren't fond of them for hanging sweaters, wire hangers are one of your most useful tools in the garden. Shape one into a rounded topiary wreath form. Cut off the hook to create "S" hooks for your hanging plants. They also make good stakes, pins, and holdfasts around the garden. The unpainted types or those with black or brown paint are the best.

Leftover Latex Paint

Interior latex paint makes good tree paint for freshly cut limbs. Latex for indoor use contains no fungicides so it's safe to apply to a fresh wound. Mix it to match the existing bark and you'll make that ugly cut portion disappear into the plant.

Military Surplus: The Commando Gardener's Spoils of War

Perhaps the most untapped supply of great gardening ideas comes from the United States military. In the past, army surplus was found at specialized stores, but today it can be found on the Internet. Formerly the design was for Vietnam and jungle warfare, which made some great items for hot, wet summer climates, but now fabrics and material are designed for the arid desert environment. Both these conditions can be found in American gardens, and the durability of this kind of wear is unmatched in the private sector. Army surplus that has been "slightly used" must be sold by the branches of service because it has no hand-me-down policy.

Fatigue Pants

Army fatigues make ideal gardening pants, comparable if not better than their consumer counterparts, the modern cargo pants, which were modeled after fatigues. But fatigues are far more durable, making exceptional working pants for the most challenging conditions. For example, they have great big pockets on the outside of each leg that are ideal for carrying clippers and other bulky items such as seed packets or bulbs. The pockets hold more due to their outside pleat. The drawstring at the bottom of each leg can be tightened to keep creepy crawlers from climbing up your legs, a great benefit in the South were bugs are epic. Unlike cargo pants, fatigues have a double reinforced seat and knees, both areas that receive hard use by gardeners sitting in the mud or on their knees to weed the beds and borders. Their loose fit allows for maximum range of motion. You can also cut off the legs to turn fatigues into equally useful summer shorts at the reinforcement seam just below the pockets and the material won't unravel.

This temporary renter's garden has a Moroccan theme featuring a tentlike shade structure created with rope and painted tree stakes. Gauzy parachute silk is large enough to create elegant seasonal shelters that offer shade without restricting air flow.

Field Jacket

This lightweight, longer-than-average jacket is a gardener's long-time favorite due to its many pockets and loose cut around the shoulders. The cut allows you to crouch and reach to the fullest extent without being constrained by the fabric and it allows you to put on lots of layers underneath. Some come with zip-out liners that offer greater warmth in the colder months, then easily adapt in spring.

Boots

Vietnam-era jungle boots evolved after the troops fighting early in that conflict found the World War II-era boot design didn't breathe and gave them foot rot. The replacement design was perfectly suited to gardeners who are always wet from calf down, particularly in areas of lots of summer rainfall. They are excellent for cleaning and grubbing rural property where you need protection from ticks and snakes. For the Southwest, military desert boots offer sturdy construction and snake protection as well.

This beautiful water garden is a temporary seasonal affair made from a lightweight resin pot that can be easily moved to storage for the winter. Growing inside is golden Acorus, water lilies, and baby water lettuce.

Parachutes

If you're looking to create a light and gauzy outdoor living space for that Lawrence of Arabia look, consider using recycled parachutes. These enormous sheets of cloth are quite affordable, particularly when you consider it's all one circular piece. The large sizes are about 60 feet in diameter; medium, about 35 feet; and smaller parachutes that were used to drop supplies average 15 feet. Nothing is as affordable for creating beautiful, light and airy shade for outdoor living areas as a parachute.

Tank Camouflage

This textile is made to cover tanks and other vehicles so they'll blend into the landscape when viewed from the air. Older forms were created out of jute rope and camouflage fabric, but today's desert camouflage nets are designed to be invisible to all kinds of space-age surveillance. They make a great tool for covering up unwanted stuff in the yard, like Uncle Joe's unfinished auto restoration project. They can also be strung on wires and poles to create visual screens that blend into the vegetation. This makes a great solution for screening off a view of the neighbor's junkyard or your window to increase privacy without wind resistance.

Ammo Boxes

Military ammunition boxes are made of strong steel, open from the top, and can be securely locked. They are priced by size from just a few dollars for smaller boxes to considerably more for ordinance. They are ideal for storing toxic garden chemicals that must be locked away from the kids, or for storing seed and other materials in a cool, dry place.

PART THREE

Gratis—As It Should Be

SOME THINGS ABOUT GARDENING WILL
never change. The most important one is that
gardening can be free or nearly so. That is proven
by our nation, built by farmers with practically
no cash and little more than a mule and a strong
back. When hard times struck during the Great
Depression and the two World Wars, it was natural
to reject those things that cost money and redis-
cover those which make our lives richer without
costing a cent. While many of these are old practices, some are new high-tech options that have
changed how information on gardening is shared,
and how gardeners actually get together.

This part of *The Small Budget Gardener* features free options to make your gardening experience more successful. Online options give anyone
with computer access the ability to tap into eons
of knowledge both written and graphic. It's also
essential to accessing nearly every seed or plant
seller without requesting a catalog by mail. This
section will close with ways Americans have fed
their families in hard times and ways the government has helped them do it.

8 Garden Tech:
Exploit the World Wide Web.

The Internet is turning economics inside out. For example, everybody on the Internet now wants stuff for free and there are so many free services available.

– Uri Geller

Over the past few centuries, gardeners gathered together in person. Those who loved plants and flowers shared their excess with friends and neighbors who lived close by. People were dependent on one another to expand their range of plants in the home garden. This community gathering gave birth to the traditional garden club, particularly during hard times when folks needed to lean on one another. Over time the garden club became a more highbrow social institution, but in the beginning it was based in practicality.

The same process is reinventing itself with the emergence of online networking. While the business community is finding similar opportunities on networking sites such as LinkedIn, the gardening world is discovering that an online garden club is equally valuable. Gardeners' networks offer opportunities to get to know others with the same interests on a local or international basis.

More recently, gardeners would save the back issues of their favorite magazines for future reference, but the Internet does this for us now in a far more efficient way. We can actually find things at a moment's notice rather than spend hours wading though back issues of *Organic Gardening* or *Better Homes & Gardens*.

Probably the biggest change seen with the advent of the Internet is the proliferation of specialty plant sellers who can finally sell direct to the consumer without paying hefty advertising fees. These plant breeders, often mom and pop companies, specialize in growing one kind of plant such as

iris or potato. They are usually able to provide you with more selection within a narrow plant type than anywhere else, and that means your garden is the better for it. This is true with heirloom plants, particularly vegetables, which may owe their very survival to Internet sales.

As the Internet grows and changes, more applications are emerging to become part of our everyday experience. How-to demonstrations were formerly restricted to television, but now there's an online video revolution where you can log on to watch sources such as YouTube show you the right way to plant a tulip. In fact, you can even film yourself planting the tulip and share that clip with the world.

As online information sources and databases mature, the worldwide knowledge of plants and gardens will grow exponentially. You as a gardener will benefit from exploring databases of accurate plant profiles, reading daily blogs of truly gifted gardener-journalists, and plugging into course materials at universities.

Online Plant Sellers

Whether you are buying from a traditional paper catalog or from an online plant seller, the basics of buying plants, seeds, bulbs, and sundries are the same. Always remember: not all companies are reputable. As many of us know all too well, it's relatively easy to get ripped off by online crooks, not to mention the possibility of identity theft. So more than ever before it is a world of *caveat emptor*, Latin for "let the buyer beware."

It's a good idea to stick with those time-tested companies that we've shopped for so long. You are assured the same quality plant materials you've received in the past and they ensure a safe shopping experience. There are lots of photos just like the catalog. They may even feature more information to help you make your purchases with greater confidence. The most beneficial feature of online shopping is the ability to search a site for exactly what you want in seconds, cutting research time down to almost nothing.

Just as other industries have associations that establish standards, the Mailorder Gardening Association (www.mailordergardening.com) is a group of the nation's best-known catalog plant sellers. Members can be relied upon for their standards of truth in advertising, customer service, and quality products. Log on to their site to find a useful clickable list of all online plant sellers in their association, which includes virtually all the good companies. Using that list, which is updated regularly, will be far more accurate and up-to-date than any addresses that can be listed in a publication. Rest assured, if they don't have it in that list, it's just not available.

There are some important guidelines for shopping online that you may want to follow when making your purchases. The guidelines ensure you get what you want, when you need it.

- Check to be sure the company's online merchant security certificate is up to date. Any site lacking a certificate will be identified with an error message on your computer. Do not provide information to this company nor make a purchase until the company is back in good standing.

The English seed house of Thompson & Morgan offers an exceptional range of plants and seeds for sale online with special Internet deals.

- Read the online catalog descriptions carefully to be sure you get exactly what you want and that it is suited to your climate. Often the best information is not immediately visible on the plant profile so be aware of highlighted "clickable" words and buttons that lead to further details on that product.
- Study your shopping cart page carefully to be sure you've got everything you need. Pay special attention to quantities because changes are often subtle and too easily overlooked online. If you have an auto-fill option on your tool bar to automatically fill in your mailing info, use it! It will save a lot of time when shopping.
- When you place an order, print out a hard copy of the order or save the order page to a file in your computer. If there's a problem with that order you'll need this data for future reference.
- If you're notified that an item is sold out, beware of allowing a substitution without prior authorization. One reason you are buying online is for the immediacy of the process. If the company isn't timely sending a sold-out notice, you may receive something wholly inappropriate.
- In all cases, order early in the season to ensure you get exactly what you want.
- If you require a specific delivery date, indicate this on your order form or with a follow-up email.
- Check for and understand the company's satisfaction guarantee policy.
- When the order is delivered, immediately check to see if it is complete and in good shape. Note that perishables such as seed potatoes from cold locations can often arrive in warm climates with frost damage.
- Plant as soon as possible. If something fails to grow, notify the nursery company immediately.

Generations of gardeners have purchased Ferry-Morse seeds. They are conveniently sold in a variety of retail locations, including home improvement, hardware, and grocery store chains.

My Gardening Catalog Address Book

To make it easier for you to access the online catalogs, the web addresses of several of some really great ones are listed here. You can photocopy this list to keep by your computer for handy reference. Just remember, web addresses change—just like people's addresses!

Abundant Life Seeds	www.abundantlifeseeds.com
Amador Flower Farm	www.amadorflowerfarm.com
Antique Rose Emporium	www.antiqueroseemporium.com
Antonelli Brothers Inc.	www.antonellibegonias.com
Big Dipper Farm	www.bigdipperfarm.com
Big John's Garden	www.bigjohnsgarden.com/
Bluestone Garden	www.bluestonegarden.com
Bluestone Perennials	www.bluestoneperennials.com
Botanical Interests Online, Inc.	www.botanicalinterests.com
Breck's	www.brecks.com
Brent and Becky's Bulbs	www.brentandbeckysbulbs.com
Brite-Lite Group	www.hydroponix.com
Brown's Omaha Plant Farms, Inc.	www.bopf.com
Burgess Seed & Plant Co.	www.eburgess.com
Burpee	www.burpee.com
Capability Simms LLC	www.aston-simms.com
Carino Nurseries	www.carinonurseries.com
Cascade Sales	www.cascadesales.com
Chamblee's Rose Nursery	www.chambleeroses.com
Charley's Greenhouse & Garden	www.charleysgreenhouse.com
David Austin Roses Ltd.	www.davidaustinroses.com/american
Deer-resistant Landscape Nursery	www.deerresistantplants.com
Dixondale Farms, Inc.	www.dixondalefarms.com
Dominion Seed House	www.dominion-seed-house.com
Doornbosch Bros. LLC	www.hollandmagic.com
Doyle's Thornless Blackberry, Inc.	www.fruitsandberries.com
Dutch Gardens	www.dutchgardens.com
Farmer Seed & Nursery	www.farmerseed.com
Field & Forests Products, Inc.	www.fieldforest.net
Garden Crossings LLC	www.gardencrossings.com
Gardener's Supply Co.	www.gardeners.com
Gardening Warehouse Direct	www.gardeningwarehousedirect.com
Gardens Alive!	www.GardensAlive.com
Gro 'N Sell Inc.	www.gro-n-sell.com
Gurney's Seed & Nursery Co.	www.gurneys.com
Harris Seeds	www.harrisseeds.com
Heirloom Roses, Inc.	www.heirloomroses.com
Henry Field Seed & Nursery	www.henryfields.com
High Country Gardens	www.highcountrygardens.com
Hobbs Farm & Greenery	www.hobbsfarm.com
Holland Bulb Farms	www.hollandbulbfarms.com
Holland Flora, LLC	www.hollandflora.com
Hoop House Greenhouse Kits	www.hoophouse.com
House of Wesley Inc.	www.houseofwesley.com

Indiana Berry & Plant Co.	www.indianaberry.com
International Greenhouse Company	www.greenhouseMEGAstore.com
Irish Eyes - Garden City Seeds	www.gardencityseeds.net
Jackson & Perkins	www.jacksonandperkins.com
Johnny's Selected Seeds	www.Johnnyseeds.com
J.W. Jung Seed Co.	www.jungseed.com
Kelly Nurseries	www.kellynurseries.com
Klehm's Song Sparrow Farm and Nursery	www.songsparrow.com
Lilypons Water Gardens	www.lilypons.com
Logee's Tropical Plants	www.logees.com
MasterGardening.com	www.mastergardening.com
Michigan Bulb Co.	www.michiganbulb.com
Miller, J.E. Nurseries, Inc.	www.millernurseries.com
Moss Acres	www.mossacres.com
Musser Forests Inc.	www.musserforests.com
National Gardening Association	www.garden.org
Nature Hills Nursery, Inc.	www.naturehills.com
New Growth	www.newgrowth.com
One Green World	www.onegreenworld.com
OnlinePlantCenter.com	www.onlineplantcenter.com
Park Seed Company	www.ParkSeed.com
PBM Group, Inc.	www.compostumbler.com
Pickering Nurseries, Inc.	www.pickeringnurseries.com
Pine Straw Direct	www.pinestrawdirect.com
Raintree Nursery	www.raintreenursery.com
Renee's Garden	www.reneesgarden.com
Rugged Country Plants	www.ruggedcountryplants.com
Santa Rosa Gardens	www.santarosagardens.com
Seeds of Change	www.seedsofchange.com
Select Seeds-Antique Flowers	www.selectseeds.com
Southern Exposure Seed Exchange	www.southernexposure.com
Spring Hill Nurseries	www.springhillnursery.com
Stark Bros. Nurseries & Orchards Co.	www.starkbros.com
Stokes Tropicals	www.stokestropicals.com
Teas Nursery Company, Inc.	www.teasnursery.com
Territorial Seed Company	www.territorial-seed.com
The Magnolia Company	www.themagnoliacompany.com
The Pepper Gal	www.peppergal.com
Thompson & Morgan Seedsmen, Inc.	www.tmseeds.com
Tulips.com	www.tulips.com
Van Bourgondien, K & Sons, Inc.	www.dutchbulbs.com
Versatile Housewares & Gardening	www.groundaug.tv
Wayside Gardens	www.waysidegardens.com
West Coast Seeds	www.westcoastseeds.com
White Flower Farm	www.whiteflowerfarm.com
Wildflower Farm	www.wildflowerfarm.com
Wildseed Farms, Ltd.	www.wildseedfarms.com
Willhite Seed Inc.	www.willhiteseed.com
Wood Prairie Farm	www.woodprairie.com
Wooden Shoe Bulb Company, Inc.	www.woodenshoe.com

Green Choices

Using paper and ink and fossil fuels in order to distribute magazines and catalogs is one of the most resource-extravagant ways imaginable to disseminate information. The sheer cost of it is not cost effective. Frankly, many of us can't afford the high cost of magazines, whose stories and pictures become has-beens in a matter of hours. Despite the fact that *The Small Budget Gardener* is a printed book, its longevity makes it a worthwhile investment. So, whenever possible, resist the temptation to use a printed catalog, and make your purchases online. In the process you'll avoid filling the landfills, and save our forests and oil.

Small-Budget Buy

Buying online is unsurpassed at offering great selection, sometimes more than any other shopping opportunity. Seeds unavailable anywhere else may be easily found online. Perennials that rarely hit the retail shelf can be common. So there is indeed the benefit of a large selection online, particularly when it comes to seed sources.

Important Factors to Consider Before Buying Online

Although you can purchase virtually any type of plant by mail, you must first consider whether it's really a good buy. Before you decide to order by mail or Internet, the truth is that a big blooming perennial in a one-gallon pot will cost about five dollars at a local garden center. When you pay the purchase price plus the hidden costs of tax, handling, and shipping, you may spend the same amount by mail or online for a small bit of root in a soil-filled baggie. Consider these important factors to determine whether buying by mail is the best choice. In many cases you'll do far better shopping at a local garden center where you can inspect the plant before you buy rather than receiving a pitiful, stressed plantlet that takes weeks just to get over its delivery shock.

Size

The overall size of the plant you want to buy dictates how easy it will be to ship. Seeds and bulbs fit nicely into a box. A tree, however, does not fit conveniently into a box and must be specially packaged to be delivered by UPS or the United States Postal Service. There will be increased cost for this packaging, which may be buried in shipping and handling. This can cause the overall price to rise, or the size of the tree may prove smaller than you expect.

Green Choices
Shipping live plants through the mail requires a tremendous amount of packaging to protect them. Cardboard boxes, plastic containers, bubble wrap, packing peanuts, and other materials are needed and all these are a waste of resources. Ultimately they must be discarded (and hopefully recycled), all to ensure a little plant can make it from California to New York in comfortable luxury.

Distance
The longer the trip, the more shipping costs are, and the longer period of time there is for a plant to suffer. Any added cost from shipping may be offset by the freedom from sales tax, but that won't help a bit if the plant arrives stressed out or dead from sitting in the freezing cold, dark, or heat for a week. It's a long trip across the country.

Shipping Costs
Postal rates are rising all the time and the cost of shipping by United States mail and other carriers can make even a small order pricey. When buying online, shipping isn't always shown clearly as it's calculated separately in some cases. Be sure you know exactly what shipping costs are because they can also include handling charges that can really drive costs higher than that of a local purchase.

Perishability
Some items such as seeds or bulbs support a huge mail order industry because they are so easy to ship with very little loss in transit. But the more sensitive a plant is to changes in its environment, the chancier it is to buy online. Even if you can return it if it's damaged, shipping a plant back to its source is not only costly but inconvenient and a poor use of fossil fuel resources.

Tightwad Gardening Tip

With ongoing budget crises, many states and cities raise their sales tax rates, which in some areas may exceed 8 percent (or more!) of your purchase! This is a substantial amount of money. Buying online from a company based outside your state can eliminate sales tax, *sometimes*. Even with shipping charges, you may still come out with some savings. Double check at the time of purchase to ensure the tax code hasn't changed (because it does); sometimes when you buy items from out-of-state companies via the Internet, no sales tax is charged. You may be able to save enough on a sizeable purchase to afford a few more items.

Local Availability

Always assess local availability before you shop online. Garden centers radically change their stock with the seasons and they know when it's time to plant in your immediate area. In high population areas, there are many garden centers to choose from so you should be able to find what you need in stock or by special order. But if you live in a more rural area where there are no garden centers, you may have no choice but to use the mail or travel to a garden center. Sometimes a long trip by car can result in bigger, better plants for less money than you'd get by mail.

Some Quality Online Seed Companies: Abundant Life Seeds; Baker Creek Heirloom Seeds; Botanical Interests Online, Inc.; Burgess Seed and Plant Co.; Burpee; Dixondale Farms; Dominion Seed House (Canada); Farmer Seed and Nursery; Garden Crossings; Gurney's Seed and Nursery Co.; Harris Seeds; Johnny's Selected Seeds; Jung Seed Company; Park Seed Company; Renee's Garden; Seeds of Change; Select Seeds — Antique Gardens; Southern Exposure Seed Exchange; Territorial Seed Co.; The Pepper Gal; Thompson & Morgan; West Coast Seeds; Wildseed Farms, Ltd.; Willhite Seed Co.; Woodprairie Farm

---

Parking

Those who live in a city must contend with circumstances that make it tough to shop for plants locally. Parking and traffic can be so discouraging that there is a high value on stress-free online shopping. If you don't have a vehicle, the benefit of home delivery is a premium. So if you're buying windowsill cacti or grow boxes for your rooftop, let the postal service worry about city traffic so you don't have to.

Seeds Online

Seeds will always be the best small-budget buy because their flat packages ship easily without risk or bulky packaging. Growing annuals and some perennials from seed costs you just pennies per plant, while that same variety may cost up to $5 in a gallon-sized container. There is always interest in new varieties, but sometimes these take a while to catch on with commercial growers. With mail order seeds you get a chance to grow them right from the start, and some seed companies even include extra free packets of seeds in gratitude for your order.

When there's an economic pinch, growing a home vegetable garden makes a lot of sense. For pennies, food plants supply us with potentially completely organic produce in a wide choice of cultivars not carried in stores. And most food plants can be sown directly into small seedling pots or into the soil making them among the least expensive food sources available.

Green Choices

All over the earth there are plant species and varieties that are disappearing forever. If they are under cultivation, some older

---

Some Heirloom Seed and Plant Sellers: The old varieties of flowers and veggies not commercially grown anymore are known as "heirlooms." Obtaining heirloom plants is the biggest reason to order online because seeds of these rarer plants aren't often found at local retailers. Many are also stable enough to save seeds to plant next year's garden. Online sellers of heirlooms include: *Antique Rose Emporium, Baker Creek Heirloom Seeds, Heirloom Roses, Native Seed/SEARCH, One Green World, Seeds of Change, Select Seeds – Antique Gardens, J.L. Hudson Seedsman*

---

varieties are being protected from extinction in seed banks, but only if the seed remains viable for a long time. Many food plant seeds such as lettuce, for example, may be viable for just one year before its germination rate decline sharply. For these plants the only hope of survival is continuous cultivation. They must be grown every year to produce seed for the following year's crop. That is the reason that companies like Seeds of Change and Native Seed/SEARCH are so important. They grow endangered food plants and sell the seed each year to keep them in continuous cultivation and thus protect them from extinction. When you plant a garden using seed from heirloom seed companies, particularly ones that have their own farms or support indigenous strains of Native American agriculture, you are contributing to the sustainability of these crops. And who knows, perhaps one of the heirlooms may prove to be the salvation of the world's food supply in times of future climate change.

Bulbs

Flower bulbs are naturally packaged into neat little units that ship easily anytime of year. In most cases it requires a lot of bulbs to create a dramatic planting, so quantity is critical. Buying bulbs in those little net bags from the garden center can add up to a considerable sum. But like anything else, when you buy in bulk from suppliers geared for such sales, you can save big on the purchase price.

With tulip bulbs, there are so many varieties they can fill botanical gardens and books with incredible options. Naturally, a supplier that imports stock from Holland will be able to offer the greatest range of choices to produce some really striking effects. So whether you are looking for loads of fragrant narcissus or that special broken 'Rococco' tulip, buying online is the very best value.

> **Top Online Bulb Sellers:** Antonelli Brothers; Brecks; Brent and Becky's Bulbs; Capability Simms; Colorblends; Dixondale Farms; Doornbosch Bros.; Dutch Gardens; Garden Crossings; Holland Bulb Farms; Holland Flora; Jackson & Perkins; Michigan Bulb Co.; Tulips.com; Van Burgondien; Wooden Shoe Bulb Co.

Roses

Roses, like seeds and bulbs, are a massive group with hundreds of cultivated varieties ranging from the ancient species to today's most flamboyant hybrid teas. The best way to buy a rose is when it is bare root and leafless and dormant. The problem for most people is that buying a rose in its leafless state makes it tough to select one based on a description on the plant tag (if it even has one). They all look virtually the same. That's why buying from catalogs or online, where you see a lot of photos and there is a lot of background information, makes it easier to make an informed choice.

Shipping bare-root roses, as well as other bare-root plants, is much easier, but only at certain times of year. The time they are shipped to you will vary from as early as January in California to much later in the North. While there are a few online plant retailers that exclusively sell roses, many of the other full-service plant sellers only sell roses for delivery during the bare-root season.

There are thousands of tulip varieties in Holland where the full range of sizes, colors, and patterns are revealed each spring.

It can be difficult to find exotic "broken" tulips such as 'Rococco' in local garden centers, but if you shop online, the whole Dutch flower bulb market turns your monitor into a European flower market.

Garden Supplies, Gifts, and Books

There are a number of very beautiful catalogs that offer all sorts of garden-related items, from tools to clothing. These are also exceptional sources of gifts, which can be pricey indeed, but are an easy way to purchase items for long distance recipients because they can be shipped directly, often with a gift card. These are exceptions to the "dead tree" approach to mail order because the printed catalogs are such a delight to the eye.

Some Top Perennial, Plant, and Tree Sellers: Amador Flower Farm; Antonelli Brothers; Big Dipper Farm; Blossom's Beautiful Plants; Bluestone Perennials; Burgess Seed and Plant Co.; Carino Nurseries; Deer-Resistant Landscape Nursery; Dixondale Farms; Dominion Seed House (Canada); Dutch Gardens; Farmer Seed and Nursery; Garden Crossings; Gro 'N Sell, Inc.; Gurney's Seed and Nursery Co.; High Country Gardens; House of Wesley, Inc.; J.E. Miller Nurseries; Kelly Nurseries; Klehm's Song Sparrow Farm & Nursery; Logee's Greenhouses; MasterGardening.com; Musser Forests, Inc.; Nature Hills Nursery; Rugged Country Plants; Santa Rosa Gardens; Spring Hill Nurseries; Wayside Gardens; White Flower Farm

Jackson & Perkins, America's best-known rose grower, has always done the majority of its business by mail because bare-root plants ship so easily.

Grootendorst roses have long been favored for their petals, which look as though they'd been cut out with pinking shears. However, this plant is rarely available outside of catalog sales.

They're jammed full of great gift ideas you can make for friends and family for pennies compared to what the catalogs charge. For this reason the added value of inspiration makes the catalog of a retailer like White Flower Farm well worth the printing.

Other garden supply catalogs are fine as online resources to find specialized equipment or tools you can't buy locally. Be aware and compare prices (including the cost of shipping heavy tools) to local alternatives. Sometimes paying more for the right tool pays off. Should you plan to add a sea of naturalized daffodils to your woodland this fall, sure, using a long-handle, foot-pushed bulb planter will cost you some money to order. But

When buying gifts for friends and relatives in far-off places, shopping online for local delivery can result in something far more appreciated than an FTD Florist bouquet.

compare that to the thousands of dollars you might spend on carpal tunnel surgery to correct damage from digging hundreds of holes with the smaller hand version of that tool.

Before you discard any outdated garden catalog, particularly

Some Top Online Rose Sellers: Antique Rose Emporium; Chamblee's Rose Nursery; David Austin Roses, Ltd.; Heirloom Roses; Jackson & Perkins; Pickering Nurseries (Canada)

those that deal with specialized types of plants, cut out the sections of how-to information. Clip the most beautiful pictures as well. Use these to create handmade greeting cards using recycled cardboard or other tactile materials. Another option is to create an old-fashioned clipping book of recipes and craft ideas. When it comes time to create something for a beloved friend, you can leaf through the pages and find a thoughtful idea to turn your summer bounty into a treasured gift.

Gardening On eBay: Pros and Cons

EBay is the online shopping site that allows everyone to be a merchant. It's so easy to sell anything online through this massive environment that it's revolutionized how people buy. Nowhere has it been more innovative than in the plant sales world, which is perfectly suited to online sales. Gardeners all over America have become amateur nurserymen, selling their extra starts and seeds online. This is a great way for any budget gardener with some knowledge and creativity to make a few extra dollars. This bypasses all the regulations of the USDA and interstate plant sales, making it much easier for buyer and seller to meet. Long live eBay for it has become a giant online garden club where free enterprise is alive and unfettered through trades, exchanges, and sales that make plants affordable to all.

Top Garden Supply, Gift, and Book Catalogs: Advance Greenhouses, Bluestone Garden, Brite-Lite Group (Canada), Burgess Seed and Plant Co., Capability Simms, Charley's Greenhouse and Garden, Dixondale Farms, Dominion Seed House (Canada), Field & Forest Products, Garden Crossings, Gardener's Supply Company, Gardening Warehouse Direct, Gardens Alive, Greenhousemegastore.com, Gurney's Seed and Nursery Co., High Country Gardens, J.E. Miller Nurseries, House of Wesley Inc., White Flower Farm

While the upside to eBay is there is no regulation, the downside is that there is no regulation. There's no way to know if you're getting what you pay for except for a small photo. Certainly the reliability rating of the seller can be helpful, but keep in mind that illegal plants are traded there, both those that are endangered and those that are downright dangerous. But with a worldwide clientele, it's as difficult to regulate as the Internet itself. From an agricultural standpoint, diseased plants could be shipped from one coast to the other spreading pathogens as they travel. But with a rapidly shrinking world, this is the future.

More Than Just Online Shopping

The Internet is without question the most important advancement to impact gardening in a century. It has certainly transformed the gardening medium from printed page to electronic screen. But its most valuable attribute is its ability to find previously obscure information about your favorite plants or ways to garden. It gives you regionally specific data that you can really use, but above all, the Internet offers interactivity.

Social Networking

With the success of My Space came the wave of social networking sites that allow folks of similar interests to come together and share online. The first sites to do this were gardener forums where questions are posted and answered by other users. While this works well, it's not the best way to get reliable information. Sites that offer professionals to moderate and answer questions are far more accurate.

The social community is more complex because it allows users to post their own profiles, pictures, videos, and blog entries, and to create specialized groups. Essentially, you get your own do-it-yourself website within this community. This is a wonderful resource, particularly in winter when gardeners resort to their communities to learn and regroup for the coming season. It is also exceptional for those with physical challenges who love plants but may not be able to garden anymore. Virtually anyone who arranges flowers, loves nature and plant photography, builds structures, or enjoys making home movies will find a home amidst the growing family of gardeners.

Top Plant Databases

It's become easy to find information on plants that's detailed, reliable, and well illustrated. No longer do you have to buy expensive reference books and sift through botanical Latin. Institutional databases give you everything you need about a plant from its shape to whether it has psychoactive alkaloids. No matter what your interest, from history to art, you'll find a database focusing on your particular interests.

> **USDA Plants:** The U.S. government database of plants, both native and exotic, cultivated and wild. http://plants.usda.gov
>
> **Learn2Grow:** Professionally written database of 90,000 plants. www.Learn2grow.com
>
> **Missouri Botanical Garden, Kemper Center for Home Gardening:** www.mobot.org

Newsletters and Blogs

Sites that want your traffic give away a ton of freebies to attract and keep your attention. They reach out in the form of newsletters, too. Some are beautifully done and illustrated while others are simple one-page formats. When you sign up for a good online newsletter that's free, you'll receive everything a resources-consuming paper publication offers but without the ecological and financial impacts. You can sign up for a blog to receive personally written material that is up to date and newsy if it's created like Garden Rant (http://www.gardenrant.com), perhaps the classiest, funniest, and most poignant of all garden blogs.

The best blogs are those written for your location. When you follow a blogger in your city, you'll hear what happens to plants if the weather hits extremes or if there's some big activity such as botanical garden plant sales of interest to gardeners in the area. Local blogs can also guide you to some great bargains and sales. The beauty of blogging and of the Internet in general is the immediacy of its information with little to no lag beween the time when you need information on how to protect your plants and when that hurricane makes landfall.

Gardening Blogs By Location

Location	Blog	URL
Alberta	Home Gardening	www.albertahomegardening.com/
Arizona	A Desert Observer	adesertobserver.blogspot.com/
California	Dirt du Jour	www.dirtdujour.com/
Hawaii	Hawaii Gardening	www.hawaiigardening.blogspot.com/
Louisiana	Growing Groceries	www.growinggroceries.com/
Maryland	Grow It Eat It	http://groweat.blogspot.com/
Michigan	In The Garden Online	http://inthegardenonline.com/main/
Minnesota	Edible Garden Landscaping	http://ediblegardenlandscaping.blogspot.com/
Montana	A Taste of Earth	http://atasteoftheearth.blogspot.com/
New England	New England Gardener	www.newenglandgardener.com/
New Mexico	A High Desert Cottage Garden	www.abqcottagegarden.blogspot.com/
New York	Cold Climate Gardening	www.coldclimategardening.com/
North Carolina	Compost Confidential	http://joegardener.typepad.com/dailycompost/
Ohio	A Study In Contrasts	http://blackswampgirl.blogspot.com/
Oklahoma	All The Dirt on Gardening	http://muskogeephoenixonline.com/blogs/MollyDay/
Oregon	Talking Plants with Ketzel Levine	www.npr.org/blogs/talkingplants/
Texas	The Laptop Gardener	http://laptopgardener.com/
Washington, DC	Calendula and Concrete	http://cc-calendula.blogspot.com/

Beautiful photos such as this one of palms can be easily printed and framed for nothing more than the price of ink, paper, and a frame.

With greeting cards sometimes costing several dollars each, you can save a lot of money, provide hours of winter crafting, and send cards whenever you wish for little more than the price of postage.

General Websites

Garden Help	www.gardenhelp.org/
Garden Rant	www.gardenrant.com
Human Flower Project	www.humanflowerproject.com/

Botanical Arts and Crafts

Old books illustrated with drawn and painted botanical drawings are incredible works of art rarely seen outside university libraries. Thankfully, the institutions that own these out-of-print works have taken the time to scan the pages and post them online. Special collections of the Missouri Botanical Garden, the Smithsonian Institute, and the USDA Special Collections are now online in full color. You can save these digital pictures in your computer to create artistic crafts. With the cost of a greeting card up to a few dollars each, it saves to create your own greeting cards using free Internet images output from your own color printer.

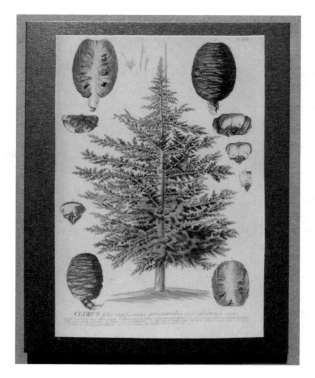

Use beautiful botanical illustrations of conifers to create one-of-a-kind holiday greetings.

The Illustrated Garden	www.illustratedgarden.org
New York Public Library	http://digitalgallery.nypl.org
Free eBook Online Botanical Illustrations	www.moplants.com

9 Making Babies:
How to propagate free plants.

"*Do you not realize that the whole thing is miraculous? It is exactly as though you were to cut off your wife's leg, stick it in the lawn, and be greeted on the following day by an entirely new woman, sprung from the leg, advancing across the lawn to meet you.*"
— Beverly Nichols, *How Does Your Garden Grow* (1935)

The development of the English cottage gardening style had its roots (so to speak) in the peasant class. They created world-class gardens through the art of plant propagation. They were the world's best budget gardeners and they didn't have a single garden center! They knew how to turn one perennial into many to fill their gardens to overflowing with exquisite blooming flowers. They even poked through the rubbish of manor houses to pocket slips and seeds of their employers, then brought home unusual plants to nurture and share with family and friends. These very simple, free, and resourceful techniques can be done by anyone so long as you know the fundamentals. Sure, you can buy many costly aids and new plants, but at the end of the day very little has changed in the age-old world of plant propagation.

The word "propagation" is the horticultural term for creating new plants. But what it means for budget gardeners is that one can acquire new plants for *free*. Once you discover how simple plant propagation can be, you'll be able to enlarge your garden without spending a penny. Chances are, the way you look at gardening will change as well. Suddenly you'll see plants everywhere in a new light, recognizing those that are suitable parent material and figuring out ways to obtain a slip or seed.

Sex in the Garden

Before venturing into the world of plant propagation, it's time for a little sex education. (Yes, you do need to read this section.) You need to understand some basic science because propagating plants isn't just a how-to; it requires some basic knowledge of genetics. Above all it is about how plants' abilities to reproduce have evolved to sustain the viability of the different species. It's also rooted in the amazing ability of plants to adapt to significant changes in the earth's climate. After all, many plants that we know as quite familiar have withstood numerous climate and environmental challenges.

This riot of diversity and abundance resulted from the cottage gardener's ability to propagate plants.

These clusters of California fan palm seed are each genetically unique, the result of pollen from a male tree and egg from the female parent (shown).

Sexual Reproduction

Plants that reproduce by seed must have pollen fertilize the egg to create a living seed. It's just like human beings and virtually all other living things. The joining of two separate gene pools shares traits that allows a plant to adapt by natural selection. Each time pollen and egg come together the seed will be unique. Sometimes the seeds of a single flower are unusually stable, and the resulting plants will be visually identical. But other plants that maintain a higher degree of variability within their species might have a crop of seed that features highly different flower colors or stature or habit. They exhibit the variability that explains why the seed you harvested from one year's red zinnias may bloom in different colors the following year.

Vegetative Propagation

Vegetative reproduction is akin to cloning. All new plants bear the same genetic code as the parent plant. This is a survival

It is very likely that every one of these wild teddybear cholla cactus are genetically identical. Every individual plant began as a section of its predecessor; each piece was detached and dropped to root where it fell.

: *This bat-faced* Cuphaea llavea *shows the proper flower shape and color for this species.*

mechanism demonstrated by the cholla cactus of the Desert Southwest. This cactus lives in such a brutal climate that its seed has little, if any, opportunity to sprout. To maintain its survival the plant bears barbed spines that are so eager to attach to a passing animal that they instantly break off the parent plant. An animal carries a cholla segment until the segment drops off and roots elsewhere, starting a whole new plant. In the California desert there are enormous stands of cholla that are all genetically identical.

The method of plant propagation you choose will be based on the species. Some species simply defy propagation no matter what method you use, or they take such a long time it's not worth the effort. Eucalyptus, for example, won't root from a cutting no matter what you do. As for the potato, there are no seeds available for most varieties but they are easily grown from a section of a tuber containing an "eye."

: *The seed offspring of the original red-colored*
: Cuphea *produced both reds and a lavender-*
: *colored bloom with uniquely colored petals.*
: *There is no guarantee what color the third*
: *generation would produce.*

Despite the fact that these cholla segments are studded with small fruits, they do not produce seed. Each segment is loosely connected to the next so it can be easily detached and carried off to root in a new location by a passing animal.

Growing Plants From Seed

Plants most often grown from seed are annuals or vegetables. Annuals are quick to sprout because they must mature, flower, and set seed all in a single growing season. This eagerness to sprout and a high rate of genetic uniformity in cultivated varieties makes them well suited to growing from seed. Some perennials are as eager to germinate, but as a rule perennials are more rapidly propagated by cuttings or divisions.

Seed is the least expensive way to raise a plant. Seed for an entire vegetable garden large enough to feed a family can be purchased for under twenty dollars. Buying seed also gives you the greatest range of plant and varietal choices. Buying seed may be the only place to find the rare and unusual plants, such as exotic gourd shapes or florist's fancy cutting sunflowers.

When you buy seed, freshness is paramount. Do not fall for sales on seed because it's false economy. Some plants produce seed that's viable for just one season while others may last a decade. If you don't know which is which, it's best to buy new seeds every year. Insist on seed that's been labeled as packed for the current year to ensure that all the seeds will sprout. Sure, if you have leftover seed you can plant them the next year, but don't stake your whole crop on these or you may be disappointed.

Always keep your seed well marked (preferably in their original packets) because without their packaging it can be nearly impossible to tell seed apart. Anyone who grows a large vegetable garden knows how quickly the little packets can accumulate in a seed drawer. In the process of sorting them out seed is spilled, packages tear, and viability is reduced overall. Store any leftover seed in tightly covered containers; mice can be a big problem that can decimate your collection over a long winter. The solution? Buy a small, heavy-duty plastic box with a tight-fitting lid. The benefit of plastic is that you can carry it into the garden when you plant. The heavy plastic is rodent proof and airtight, which will retain seed viability for as long as possible. One propagation expert advises to stuff the seed envelopes into mason jars with banded lids to keep them perfectly airtight.

Collecting Seed

You can buy your seed, collect them from your plants, or share with friends. The problem is, we don't often allow our plants to go to seed because this stops flower and fruit production. It usually spells the demise of a plant because seed production signals the end of the season. Should seed be available on the plant, wait until the

If you begin to notice which plants are producing seed in your neighborhood, it will amaze you how much is out there that just goes to waste.

seedpod or capsule is fully mature and beginning to open on its own to release the seed. Collect individual seeds or the entire pod, sift out the debris, and store in a cool, dry place to plant the following year. Look for seed in your own garden, along the wayside, or in friends' yards where plants have been allowed to finish their annual cycle. Homes that are old abandoned homesites are great places to pick up free seed. Most plants flower and produce seed annually, particularly when under stress from neglect. Sometimes you'll find a forgotten heirloom treasure or a little known contemporary variety with seed galore.

Tightwad Gardening Tip

Ask for a flat whenever you buy bedding plants at the garden center. This is a lot like asking for the hanger when you purchase clothing; you can use it again and again at home. Those flats with a nearly solid or perforated bottom are more desirable because they can hold soil. Those with an open lattice bottom may require a lining of newspaper or weed barrier fabric to contain soil. Either way, this is a free bonus you'll use many times over.

Sowing Seed In Pots and Flats

Every spring millions of wildflowers resow themselves across America, and for some it seems a million more sprout as weeds in the garden. Sowing seed should be just that simple if you follow a few important guidelines on containers, soil, and aftercare.

Containers can make it much easier to grow from seed because you're better able to control moisture in the root zone. Nurseries have always used

  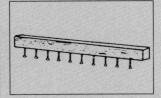

Left: *If you are making your own seedbed soil, it's a good idea to build a wood frame sieve using ¼-inch hardware cloth for the metal grid. This allows you to fill flats directly from the sieve, ensuring soil that is light and free of rocks, sticks, and hard dirt clods.* **Center:** *Once the seed is in place, it's essential that you cover it with the right amount of soil. Very small seed may require only 1/16 inch of soil to cover it, which is difficult to do by hand. Simplify this by filling an old mayonnaise jar with soil. Poke holes in the lid with a nail and screw the lid back onto the jar. Then simply shake out the soil as you would salt, in a thin but much more evenly applied layer.* **Right:** *To make evenly spaced depressions in a seedbed, create a guideline bar. Use a 2-by-2-inch wood segment to create a bar from 12 to 18 inches long. Pound a series of nails into the bar securely at regular intervals. Turn it over with the nail heads facing downward and press it into a flat of soil; you'll be able to space your seeds more accurately.*

flats, which are shallow square trays filled with soil just a few inches deep. These are sown with seed at regular intervals to get as many plants started as possible. Sowing in a single flat or similar container makes it much easier to keep the seedbed in ideal germination conditions than it is lots of small containers. Once they've sprouted, the seedlings are later potted up into individual containers.

You don't have to start your plants in flats; virtually anything that holds soil can be put to use. Here is a list of common items that you might otherwise throw away. If a container is plastic, be sure to make drain holes with a hot coathanger, screwdriver, or nail.

Cat litter box
Underbed storage box
Tin casserole dish
Fruit crate
Disposable aluminum baking pans
Tin loaf pan
Silverware organizers

Deeper containers can be used for seedlings as well as rooting cuttings and for other forms of plant propagation.

Refrigerator crisper drawer
Galvanized wash tub

Green Choices

Clear plastic containers are used today to sell fruit, salads, sandwiches, and many other types of fresh food. They are perfect for sprouting seed of all kinds. The size is ideal for a windowsill to start your garden well ahead of the season. Those types with the hinged lids feature small holes for air circulation. Line the bottom with paper to keep the soil in place. Just imagine how much greener our world would be if every one of these were reused to grow seedlings!

A great way to start veggie seedlings is with egg crates and egg flats that offer perfectly sized cells for seeds to germinate.

Planting one or two seeds per cell allows for an occasional germination failure.

Simple Steps to Successful Seedbed Germination

- Buy finely textured, light seed-growing soil to avoid too wet, too dry, or infected seedbeds.
- Use smaller pottery shards, pea gravel, or very coarse sand in a layer on the bottom of containers to aid drainage.
- Plant the seed exactly at the depth indicated on the package. If you don't have the seed package plant all seed at a depth twice that of the seed's diameter.
- Use a seedling bed marker to create rows and help designate proper intervals.
- Cover seed with very light material such as compost that won't pack down.
- Put soil in a kitchen strainer or poke holes in the lid of a jar to create a "salt shaker" to help you cover your seed evenly.
- Water with a misting nozzle to avoid dislodging seed or risk washing it out.
- If the seed medium resists absorbing water, set that container inside a larger one and fill the larger one with water to half as high as the container's rim. Allow the container holding the seed medium to sit until its surface is uniformly wet via a wicking process; then remove the container and drain.

A whole vegetable garden sits growing in a sunny room until the weather warms outside.

The Poor Gardener's Greenhouse

A cold frame is no more than a glass-topped wooden box that insulates seedlings or cuttings from extreme temperatures and dehydration. Any serious gardener should have one because it does the temporary spring job of a greenhouse without the expense. Plus, when you've got a wide range of seedlings, there's rarely enough room on a windowsill to start them all.

The cold frame's glass (or clear plastic) top should

This fancy built-in cold frame utilizes brick insulation on the back and side.

be angled in one direction, typically toward the south. This also indicates that the location of the cold frame must have an unobstructed south-facing exposure to be the most functional. Inside the cold frame seedlings remain warm and moist through the often chilly nights of spring. As the seedlings mature, they are hardened off (acclimated to the outside temperatures) gradually by cracking open the cold frame window an inch at a time until they can survive all night with it fully opened.

When an old-fashioned cold frame was heated, it became a hotbed. This is a wonderful, organic idea that utilized the heat of decomposing manure, which is much like the heat generated at the center of a compost pile. At the bottom of the cold frame a farmer would spread a thick layer of very fresh manure, then cover this with seed-starting soil. Seed was planted directly into this medium, which was warmed from the bottom up by the decomposing manure. This mimicked the warm ground of early summer, which is a trigger for seeds to germinate and seedlings to mature much faster.

Buying Seedbed Soil Pays

One area you don't want to scrimp on is seedbed soil. This is because so many organisms can linger there to infect new seedlings. When you purchase well-sterilized seed-starting medium that offers the ideal mix of material and water-holding potential, your germination rates will skyrocket.

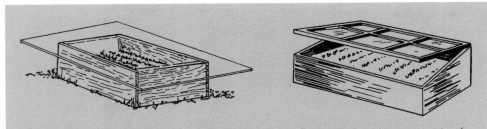

Left: *One of the simplest ways to create a cold frame for germinating seed or encouraging cuttings to root consists of a wooden box with a sheet of tempered glass set directly on top. Tempered glass is much safer. If it breaks because it disintegrates into small pieces.* **Right:** *This traditional cold frame utilizes a six-pane window attached to a wooden box with a hinge. Notice how the top of the box is slanted. A cold frame should face south to allow more direct sunlight to reach its interior.*

The traditional-style cold frame begins with an old salvaged window in its frame or sash. These are widely available at house demolition storage yards. Avoid any with cracked glass or panes because rain will seep through them to wash away seed inside the cold frame. The box is usually built to the dimensions of the window, so there are no standard dimensions. A well-built combination of window and box can be quite attractive, particularly if it's painted and finished with attractive hardware. But budget gardeners don't always have such luxury. If you can find an existing wood box it saves a lot of money on materials and labor. The window can be larger than the box but it cannot be smaller or there will be gaps where cold air and weather may enter. One of the best ways to get started is to use a pine shipping box. Another option is to start with a wooden crate and enclose the gaps between the crate slats with plywood. Utilize all found or salvaged wood for the cold frame to make it as close to free as you can. Even if it is rather unattractive, so long as it works the seedlings won't care one bit.

For real tightwads and where you need more insulation, a straw bale cold frame is the perfect solution. This should be considered a temporary solution that may last a few years or more depending on your local climate. Straw bales are strong enough to stand on their own and provide some of the best insulation possible. Gardeners in the far north are building straw bale houses, sheds, and greenhouses by stacking bales and connecting them with metal reinforcing bars (rebar). There are online resources for many types of straw bale construction for those on a budget at www.strawbale.com and other sustainable building material websites.

A straw bale cold frame need only be one bale tall with a large window placed on top. For best results, create a frame around the window that can be raised to sit at an angle for proper solar exposure. For very large straw bale cold frames use sliding glass doors (tempered glass for safety) in metal frames. In damp climates, cold frame straw bales may be taken apart after planting the garden to be used for mulch in summer or winter.

Protecting Seedlings from Late Spring Cold Snaps

When a little seedling is transplanted outdoors into garden soil it can experience wind, heat, cold, and possibly a light frost. Hungry pests seeking spring greens can consume seedlings before they have a chance to grow. These problems are faced by every gardener, and over the years many ingenious attempts have been made to solve this problem. While there are all sorts of bed coverings and plant bells you can buy to protect plants, there are many ways to achieve the same result without spending a dime.

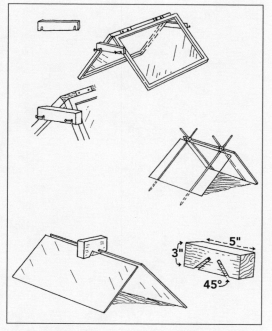

English gardeners developed this method of creating miniature portable greenhouses out of picture frames or small, single windows of similar size. These are used for propagation and to help shelter seedlings in spring and fall (right side illustration). **Top:** *In order to make a portable picture frame greenhouse sturdier, simply create a crossbar out of wood and secure it with two nails as shown.* **Middle:** *To use window panes or glass that lacks a wood or metal frame, lash together sticks to support the underside of the glass. If the edges of the glass are sharp, carefully cover them with a thin strip of duct tape.* **Bottom:** *Here's another way to support two similar-sized panes or unframed glass. The 3-by-5-inch block of wood simply clips the top edges together.*

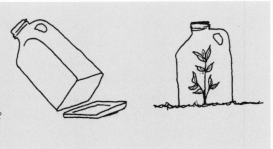

To create a simple seedling protector, cut the bottom off a plastic half-gallon or gallon milk jug. Poke holes in the lid or remove the lid entirely to ensure that there is sufficient oxygen inside.

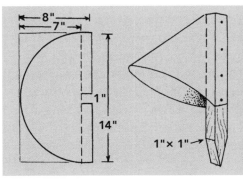

Cut stiff plastic sheeting or Mylar into a semicircle, as shown in this photo. Attach it to a one-inch stake 10 to 12 inches long to create an adjustable protective cover.

You can use a gallon, half-gallon, or even a quart wide-mouth jar or heavy plastic container to protect seedlings and cuttings. Simply turn the container over and set it down over the plant. Be sure to prop it up on one edge to allow air circulation.

From WWII England came a way to protect seedlings in rows from cold and even snow. Don't pass up wood picture frames (with glass) at the next garage sale if they can be purchased in pairs. Take two frames about the same size and attach them along one side with a hinge attached to the wooden part of the frame, or even use a strip of duct tape. Place this miniature A-frame over a row of seedlings and, like the A-frame cabin design that easily sheds snow, your miniature cold frame is the ideal protection from an early summer hail storm.

You can use jars to cover single seedlings but jars do not offer the option of allowing air to pass through. A better option is to cut the bottoms off plastic milk jugs. Remove the cap to ensure there is plenty of air circulation inside and to release excess heat that will build during the day.

Other types of coverings on a larger scale can extend the harvest into fall. The simplest method is a Quonset-style covering made of corrugated fiberglass and stakes of salvaged PVC pipe, galvanized pipe, or wood to hold it in place. Hoop-style greenhouses are an excellent choice as well and, though they can be made from scratch with ½-inch PVC arches and plastic sheeting, buying reusable types is well worth the expense.

In the Midwest, avid gardeners rely on greenhouses for their winter veggies. Many people have created entire structures of stacked straw bales that are plastered with stucco on the outside. Not only are they thick, sturdy, and inexpensive, the insulation factor is unbeatable. In this simplified version of that idea, straw bales are stacked into two walls and thick plastic sheeting or corrugated fiberglass roofing panels are laid over the top. The following season you can till the straw into the soil or use it as mulch.

Growing New Plants From Cuttings

The majority of all woody plants are vegetatively propagated by cuttings. In concept the process is simple: cut off a part of one plant, allow it to grow roots, and then plant the cutting somewhere else. In reality it is more complex because each kind of plant differs in its willingness to grow roots. For example, willows seem to root the moment a cutting touches ground while a eucalyptus refuses to root under any circumstance. This variability makes propagation from cuttings tricky and whole books have been written about the individual preferences of different species.

To extend the harvest for vegetable crops, stake a panel of corrugated fiberglass roofing in place as shown. It is surprisingly durable and will even withstand a light snowfall. Later in the fall you can store the corrugated panels flat and out of the way under your house, beneath a deck, or in the rafters of the garage.

For budget gardeners who don't want to spend more to increase the number of plants they have, get started with the basics. A typical cutting is composed of cells that create stem tissues. It must generate entirely new cells that create root tissues before roots can form. That requires the use of hormones, which the cutting must provide itself before the change can occur. One reason there are rooting powders for sale is to eliminate the need for a cutting to generate hormones itself. These powders are actual hormones you apply to the cut site to stimulate cell change. In essence they eliminate the hardest job of the cutting so it can immediately get started generating root cells before it dies of dehydration.

Propagation by cuttings is divided into two basic types: hardwood and softwood. These distinctions relate to the kind of stem material you use as well as the season in which the cutting is taken. They also differ in the time it takes the cutting to produce roots.

Rooting media can vary considerably depending on what you have on hand. Many budget gardeners salvage leftover masonry sand from construction sites because so little is needed in propagation. Simply wash the sand well to remove any excess dust or contaminants. The type of sand called "sharp sand" tends to leave lots of air spaces between very large particles that ensures there's enough oxygen around the cutting to support roots. If sharp sand is not available, pure sand gathered from deserts, riverbeds, and freshwater lake beaches is a fine substitute. Do not use ocean sand or sand in any way colleted near a saltwater body as it will produce conditions too alkaline to support plant life. The same applies to roadside sands and gravels where salt is used in winter. Other store-bought mediums for plant propagation include vermiculite and perlite, which make excellent substitutes.

Geraniums are one of the simplest perennials to root from a softwood cutting.

Learning the Ropes: Rooting Geraniums

Step 1: Take a tip cutting and remove all but the top few leaves. (Optional: Dip the cut end into rooting powder.)

Step 2: Insert the cutting into the rooting medium if you're using one, and cover the cutting with an inverted glass or plastic container to reduce dehydration. Be sure to allow some gaps around the bottom for air exchange.

Step 3: After two weeks, check the cutting frequently for signs of root development. When a number of new roots are showing, it is ready to be planted into soil.

Step 4: Plant the newly rooted cutting in a flowerpot and keep moist until ready to plant outdoors. Be sure to acclimate new plants gradually to avoid shock.

Softwood Cuttings

Many perennials and evergreen shrubs are propagated by softwood cuttings. Softwood cuttings are taken during the growing season when plant tissue at the tip of a twig or branch is still green and soft. The old test for the ideal quality of a softwood cutting states that, "The shoot will snap clean across instead of bend or only partially break." This ensures a cutting is rapidly growing and therefore more inclined to root, but at this time of year cuttings are most vulnerable to dehydration. Softwood cuttings require plenty of warmth, preferably a constant temperature.

The ideal length for a softwood cutting is from 3 to 6 inches long. It's best to remove all but a few leaves at the top to help speed rooting. Apply rooting hormone to the cut end, then insert the cuttings into your rooting medium. Stiff stems can simply be pushed down into the medium, leaving one or two buds

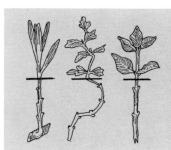

These are three examples of different types of softwood cuttings with leaves and stems removed from the underground portions. The lines show how deep cuttings should be positioned in the rooting medium.

and the leaves aboveground. If the stems are soft, use a dibble or a piece of wood of similar diameter to make a hole, then gently place the cutting at the correct depth and tamp the medium down around it.

Since softwood cuttings are actively growing when they are taken, they will lose moisture quickly. Keep them well shaded and evenly moist but not so wet that drainage is compromised or mildew appears. Strive for a constant temperature at an optimal 55 to 65 degrees F, and give tropical plants even warmer conditions. As cuttings begin to grow more vigorously after one week to a month, depending on the species, gradually remove the shading or they will become weak and spindly. Check their progress often by digging out a cutting; once roots form, transplant into nutritious, finely textured potting soil.

Hardwood Cuttings

These old roses found growing in a cemetery can be easily propagated by layering for a risk-free start in your garden.

Except for roses, this method of plant propagation is not well suited to beginning gardeners. Hardwood cuttings are typically taken from one-year-old twigs that are strong and firm, with no signs of withering. Growers take cuttings in fall before the ground freezes, placing them into deep wooden boxes filled

with coarse sand for the winter. There they sit, gradually producing a callus, which is a hard, scablike growth that takes many
months to develop. In spring the callused cuttings are lifted
from the sand and planted out in garden soil or in pots before
temperatures warm. They will then quickly begin producing roots
once temperatures rise.

The size of a hardwood cutting can vary from a few inches to
a foot in length, with diameters averaging about that of a pencil.
Cuttings must have at least two buds, one for top growth and
one for root development, but more buds are recommended to
compensate for loss or damage. To make sure you always know
which end is up with these barren twigs, cut the bottom end on
an angle and the top end on a square. The pointed end also
makes it easier to press the cutting into the rooting medium.

Cutting Environment

For simple and more successful propagation by cuttings, it's
helpful to have a greenhouse, a cold frame, a hot bed, or simply a box covered with glass. Cuttings of all sorts root far better
where there is heat beneath their rooting medium.

The budget gardener will discover that mild bottom heating
will occur if you place the rooting containers on a shelf above a
heater vent, wood stove, or kitchen stove. But the rising heat can
prematurely dry cuttings, particularly softwood cuttings, unless
they are protected by a greenhouse-like environment. Therefore,
cover them with a layer of plastic or a plastic milk jug or some
other structure to create a moister mini-environment.

Layering: Foolproof and Risk Free

Layering is a method of propagation that allows you to root a
portion of an existing plant easily and without risk. It has traditionally been the method of propagating vines because the
long runners of vines are genetically programmed to root when
they touch the ground. Sometimes the runner is covered with a
layer of litter on the forest floor, and there the perfect conditions
cause it to root. A vine in the wild can layer itself to cover a vast
area, which is how blackberry thickets evolve.

When layering vines, you're simply recreating this same
scenario in the garden. Layering can be used for other kinds
of plants provided they have limbs long enough to reach the
ground. Or you can rig up pots to bring the ground to the limb if

The People's Problem Solvers

Some woody plants are so quick to produce roots they become a problem, which is the case with Lombardy poplar and the American cottonwood. These were a homesteader's best friends and are equally beneficial to a cash-strapped gardener or landscaper who has a good-sized homesite that needs shade and beauty.

These plants come from genus *Populus* named for the fact that these were the "people's tree" and they are still that today. They can grow into enormous trees from a small cutting planted directly into the soil with little assistance or worries about climate. These water-loving trees produce a fine network of smaller roots that could quickly fill a grower's nursery pot in what seemed like weeks after a rootless cutting was pressed into the container soil. After testing, it was determined that poplars would perform better if they were planted in a deep but narrow hole from a giant-sized cutting or pole. When planted during

Poplars are among the best trees to propagate with dormant cuttings and poles.

the bare-root season in a posthole, some poplars have produced incredible trees due to their far larger root system. In a posthole they sprout roots around the entire portion of the underground cutting. The aboveground portion, which is from three to ten feet tall at planting, can add well over five feet of growth per year, offering a vital problem solver for protecting crops, creating a windbreak, creating shade, conserving energy, and growing firewood.

To cash in on these popular freebies, find the poplar trees in your neighborhood. There are many different species of poplar in cultivation from Asia, Europe, and North America. Those planted in newer parks may be the desirable cottonless cottonwoods that are superior sources for cuttings. Choose a parent plant that provides the characteristics you want, then negotiate with the owner to cut some whips or poles, preferably base suckers or water sprouts that should come out anyway. Then plant the cuttings and from there populate your entire homesite for free.

This method may also work well for willows, birch, and alder, all of which prefer similar moist conditions.

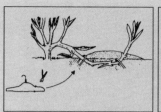

Most vines or other plants that are sufficiently flexible can be propagated by layering. **Left:** *Step 1 — Bend down a lower branch of the plant. Nick the bottom of the limb to encourage rooting and add hormones if you wish. Place the branch in a small groove in the soil and anchor the limb in the soil with giant "bobby pins" made of wire coat hangers. Cover the remainder of the limb with sand or soft topsoil.* **Center:** *Step 2 — Check the limb after a few weeks for signs of rooting. During warm months this may occur quickly, but during cold weather it can take many months. When the damaged portion begins to show sufficient rooting, cut it off the mother plant. Many believe you should sever the limb but wait a week before transplanting the newly rooted part because severing and transplanting at the same time can unnecessarily stress the new plant.* **Right:** *Another method of layering allows you to place the new plant in a pot right from the start. Then when you sever it from the mother plant there is no need for transplanting.*

conditions allow. This is the ideal way for a beginner to expand a garden for virtually no cost whatsoever.

To layer a plant, select a long branch or runner that can come in contact with the soil at least a foot back from the growth tip. That tip will soon become the new plant. At the point where the branch or runner touches the ground take a knife and gently scrape away the bark but don't gouge the surface deeply. This will encourage callus material to form, or you can apply rooting hormone to those moist tissues to speed things along. Then place the cut portion in direct contact with the soil in a way that does not produce undue tension on the base or the tip of the runner. One way could be to peg it into place with a giant bobby pin made out of a wire coat hanger. Mound sand or compost over the break and leave it for a month or two. If you're layering in fall leave it for the entire winter. Since it is still connected to the mother plant there is no real concern for the welfare of a cutting.

For plants that naturally layer themselves such as chrysanthemums, spider plants, or berry vines, roots may develop in a matter of weeks. Check to see if they've started, and if so, sever the runner from the parent behind the point of rooting. Allow the now independent new plant to continue rooting in the same location so it can stabilize on its own. Then feel free to transplant to a pot or other new location.

Plants Suitable to Layering

Chrysanthemum	Tomato	Honeysuckle	Heather
Virginia Creeper	Weeping Willow	Roses, climbers, and ramblers	Creeping Rosemary
Morning Glory	Mulberry	Lantana	Passionflower
Spider Plant	Clematis	Grapevines	Trumpet Creeper

The Ease of Propagating Succulents

What makes succulents so easy to propagate is that they retain water in their body parts and are therefore less dependent on their roots to obtain water. In fact, some succulents can be severed from the parent plant and survive without roots for up to two years, yet still retain enough energy to root and grow. This makes succulent gardens the easiest and least expensive of all budget landscaping endeavors.

Succulents aren't all from warm regions such as southern Africa or Mexico. There is an enormous group of them that grow high atop mountains in the alpine world. These are remarkably

This rare double wisteria may be hard to find for sale, but a local specimen can easily be rooted by layering.

Beautiful tropical vines naturally layer themselves in the litter of a jungle floor.

cold hardy for a succulent and seem to defy winters with their very survival. Yet they need those succulent parts to survive the poor granular soils of high elevations where they thrive in nooks and crannies on rocky mountainsides. These are for the most part species in the genuses *Sedum* and *Sempervivum*, which are just as easy to propagate as tender succulents.

Among the succulents is the large family of cacti, which are native to the Americas and bear some of the most wicked spines in the entire plant kingdom. Propagating cacti can be one of the easiest ways to make more plants so long as you are careful. The prickly pear group not only have large spines but bear nearly microscopic glochids. Glochids look like fine hairs but are actually very sharp and so tiny they're impossible to extract from the skin if they break off. To handle cacti it's wise to obtain a sturdy set of barbecue tongs, some heavy welder's gloves, and a few pieces of carpet that you can wrap around the cactus when you are moving large plants or cuttings. Keep the cuttings separated from one another so they don't puncture another's delicate skin, which will develop a wound that never completely disappears.

These alpine plants of the genus Sempervivum *produce daughter rosettes connected by fleshy stems to the mother plant. They are easy to sever and root into new plants.*

The long, flexible limbs of weeping willow can easily be layered as can weeping cherries and mulberry.

....
*This Kalanchoe is a
succulent that pro-
duces tiny plantlets
around the edges of
its mature leaves. They
naturally fall to the
ground and root, or
they may be picked off
and rooted.*

If you live where cacti and succulents grow freely, be it deserts or mountaintops, starting to propagate your own leads to
discovering free plantlets everywhere you look. This is a wonderful form of gardening that anyone can do provided they remember that the chief enemy of these plants is heavy soils and poor
drainage. Err on the side of too porous soil at the expense of
fertility to stay on the safe side.

Succulents share a unique ability to create offsets or "pups,"
which are a way to vegetatively reproduce themselves in climates
too barren to support seedlings. Pups are designed by nature to
easily separate from the parent plant and take root where they
fall. You can separate pups and root them easily in sand as they
are already programmed to root at these locations, more so than
a more traditional cutting.

The most important rule of a cactus or succulent cutting is that
it must have time to dry the wound before you plant it into any soil
or rooting medium. Succulent tissues are sterile, and if exposed
to earth while still open and moist, pathogens can enter the plant
to begin the rot process. Even though it is counterintuitive, leave
your cuttings to air-dry for a few days so the wound can harden
before inserting the cutting into rooting medium. Sand remains
the best medium for rooting all types of succulent plants.

Plant Division

The ever-popular perennials are the group that is most often included in the propagation technique called "division." This process renews the mother plant and yields lots of new ones to spread around the garden. This is why a perennial is such a good buy; thrifty folks know one plant will soon become many. Each kind of perennial has its own optimal season for division, but you can cheat and divide anytime if need be. This is important when you see landscapers working in the neighborhood because an older perennial dug up to make way for a new plant can yield a wealth of free plants no matter when it happens.

Prior to division a plant must be "lifted" or dug up, which is often done with the spading fork because it does not sever the roots like a shovel does. An old technique uses two garden forks, each set opposite the other with the tines set deep into the soil beneath the plant between them. When both forks are pushed down the plant pops out, nice and clean. Once the plant is out of the ground use a garden hose to clean the soil from the roots to get a good look at how the plant is growing.

Each segment of prickly pear cactus can be cut at a joint to start a new plant.

This established stand of agapanthus can yield hundreds of new plants if they're dug and divided.

You'll likely see the remnants of the original plant and lots of growth points around it that have spread outward over the years. These may have roots of their own, meaning they are ready to be cut away from the parent and replanted. When it's out of the ground a perennial is vulnerable and the pieces must be replanted or potted up as soon as possible so the roots don't dry out. Very small, weak plants, or those with few or no roots, may be potted and nurtured over winter to plant in spring. Those with hardier segments can go right back into the ground.

Knowing which plants are easiest to divide and the best time of year to do so is important to their survival. The optimal season to divide will vary by one's local climate. If the division period is indicated as early spring, that means divide at the first signs of growth.

These professional propagators are dividing perennial mother plants into many new slips that will be potted up for sale.

Fall or spring division takes advantage of rapid growth in these in-between seasons. Others must be divided after they flower so you need not sacrifice the blooms in a division year.

The Most Easily Divided Perennials by Genus

Genus	Common Name	Best Time to Divide
Achillea	Yarrow	Fall
Agapanthus	Lily of the Nile	Early spring
Anemone	Anemone	After flowering
Armeria	Thrift	After flowering
Asparagus	Asparagus	Spring
Bellis	English Daisy	After flowering
Chrysanthe-mum	Chrysanthemum	Fall or spring
Coreopsis	Tickseed	Spring
Delphinium	Larkspur	Early spring
Dicentra	Bleeding Heart	Early spring
Echinacea	Purple Coneflower	Fall or spring
Geum	Geum	Early spring
Hemerocallis	Daylily	Fall or spring
Heuchera	Coral Bells	Spring
Kniphofia	Red Hot Poker	Early spring
Lupinus	Hybrid Lupine	Early spring
Nepeta	Mint	Early spring
Oenothera	Evening Primrose	Fall or spring
Rudbeckia	Black-eyed Susan	Fall or spring
Salvia	Sage	Fall or spring
Thymus	Thyme	Fall or spring
Vinca	Periwinkle	Early spring

It's easy to divide dahlias. First, dig up the cluster of tubers that surrounds the roots and store it until spring. Then, sever each one very carefully so it has a portion of the stem attached that bears a growth eye. The eye is the source of next year's plant. Any tuber cut without a growth eye will fail. Replant each of the severed tubers in spring.

Bulbs, Rhizomes, Corms, and Tubers

Bulbs are one of the easiest plants to propagate because they automatically multiply underground. A mature bulb or corm will produce pea-sized bulblets all around the mother. Traditionally you'll dig up the adult and replant without its bulblets to ensure flowers in the following year are just as big and beautiful. If a bulb is left in the ground the bulblets will grow slowly and produce many nonflowering or poorly flowering plants, which can spoil the look of the mother plant.

To propagate the bulblets into full-sized bulbs like the growers do, you must dig them up and separate them. Then replant the little ones in a holding area of the garden where you can give them optimal conditions so they grow and mature. Once they reach full size a couple of years later, you'll have full-sized bulbs.

The most noteworthy tuber is the dahlia, which develops a cluster of fleshy roots shaped like small sweet potatoes that radiate out from a central point like spokes on a wheel. In cold climates dahlia tubers must be dug up and stored for winter and they are divided just before replanting in spring. Carefully cut the tubers away from the central stalk taking care that each one has a bit of stem attached. The stem is where the growth eyes are located and an eye must be present or the tuber won't grow. Potatoes are another example of tubers that must have a growth eye to ensure they grow.

A rhizome is simply a long stem that grows underground to help a plant spread out and root into new plants. Many types of grasses spread by rhizomes. Some plants like cannas or German iris produce

Newly divided plants are replanted into these rich propagation fields to develop more solid roots.

fleshy rhizomes. They are easy to propagate by severing the rhizomes at a growth point and replanting elsewhere.

Stolons are like rhizomes that grow aboveground. Strawberries are a typical example of this kind of plant that produces daughter plants at the end of a stolon. Bermuda grass is also an aggressive spreader, producing roots at shoots at regular intervals along the stolon. These plants are all the easiest to propagate simply by severing the stolon and replanting.

Green Choices

Local gardening organizations become community clearinghouses for surplus plants and bulbs after members divide their own plants. Anyone with a million yellow daylilies is likely to discard the fruits of division, which they often share with other community members. Garden clubs, once quite popular, have lost their prominence and have been replaced by more ecological groups such as native plant societies or friends of botanical gardens and wildland parks. Becoming involved in these environmentally focused groups can ensure you'll be the receiver of all sorts of surplus plants, many of which can be potted and sold to raise money for conservation efforts.

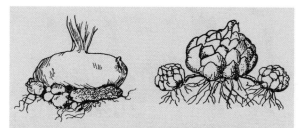

Left: *Corms (such as gladiolus) and true bulbs develop babies around their fleshy root structures each year. If they are dug up and split off, you can create many new free plants. The babies may require a year or two of tender care to develop into mature, blooming adults.*
Right: *Lilies develop long roots, which support new babies. When lilies are dug up for winter, simply sever the long roots to free the new babies and nurture them for a season or two until they mature.*

Tightwad Gardening Tip

Seas of daffodil bulbs are often one of the few lingering vestiges of long-forgotten homesteads. They are also survivors in old graveyards because they are one of the few plants not decimated by gophers or other pests due to their inherent toxicity. If you find such botanical artifacts, contact the landowner and ask to dig up a few. It won't hurt the remaining plants and you can propagate your gleanings into a large family of your own.

To obtain many new plants from an overgrown patch of bearded iris, you must dig up the fleshy roots. Break apart each segment or cut cleanly at a natural joint that bears a growing tip. Allow the cut ends a day or so to harden off before replanting so there is less chance for rot to set in. Plant as deep as the roots were when you first dug them.

10 Eat for Free:
Your backyard veggie superstore.

"The first gatherings of the garden in May of salads, radishes and herbs made me feel like a mother about her baby—how could anything so beautiful be mine. And this emotion of wonder filled me for each vegetable as it was gathered every year. There is nothing that is comparable to it, as satisfactory or as thrilling, as gathering the vegetables one has grown."

— Alice B. Toklas

When times are hard and money is tight, folks always return to the garden. It has historically been the salvation of families and whole communities during times when traditional sources of food have been interrupted. Such was the case during World War II when the Victory Garden not only helped with the war effort, but it provided better nutrition for young and old. Even before that, during the Great Depression, a backyard food garden was a necessity, and wherever there was a plot of land a homeowner or renter cultivated it to stretch his income.

Today these same needs are augmented by the desire for pure food uncontaminated by genetic modification or chemicals. While certified organic produce does solve these problems, its higher cost is now beyond many family budgets. In times of economic downturn, the best way to feed a family with pure nutritious food is to grow it yourself. While this concept may be new to many, budget gardeners have always grown seasonal gardens.

Large, fast-growing vines of squash and melons require a great deal of space.

Understanding the Food Garden

The backyard veggie "superstore" is far more than the typical food garden of seasonal tomatoes and squash. It's the idea of evaluating your entire homesite for its overall productivity. This potential includes a large range of permanent plants such as trees, shrubs, and vines that yield prolific crops of delicious food year after year. There are beautiful herbs and perennials that offer flavoring and edible flowers as well as delicious shoots and roots every year. The key to saving money is to make an investment in these long-term plants in lieu of strictly ornamental ones so your landscape is productive as well as beautiful.

The way to get started is to narrow your plant choices according to plant longevity. This allows you to easily see what should be a permanent part of your garden and what will be ephemeral, which means it's here today and gone tomorrow.

Perennial food plants such as these artichokes thrive amidst the flowers.

Annuals

Annuals grow from seed, mature, produce seed (sometimes in the form of fruit), and die all in one season. Most traditional vegetable crops are annuals, which is why a majority of them are grown from seed each year. They can also be bought as seedlings. Annual food plants offer different edible parts such as fruit, leaves, roots, and stems. The area where you grow annuals is typically set aside from the rest of the garden because it requires extensive annual soil preparation to keep soil fertility at its highest level as these are heavy feeding plants. The vegetable garden may not be particularly attractive because it's purely functional and is designed each year to rotate crops.

Grow these annuals from seed: corn, squash, lettuce, beans, greens, carrot, radish, cucumber, melon, peas, and sunflower.

Grow these annuals from seedlings to get a head start on the harvest: tomato, pepper, broccoli, and eggplant.

Perennials

Perennial plants that produce food are permanent parts of the landscape. Often it takes a couple of years to raise a highly productive bed, but once established it produces year after year without needing to be replanted. Good examples of a perennial food crop are asparagus, artichokes, and strawberries. There are not nearly as many perennials as annuals in the food garden, but these are a budget gardener's dream because you need not buy seedlings or seed each year to get a harvest.

Woodies

Trees, shrubs, and vines are plants that produce woody parts such as a trunk or twigs. Woody plants are the slowest of all plant categories to mature and produce food, but they are without question the most long-lived. A fruit tree can last for decades and grapevines are world renowned for their long lifespan. The beauty of woodies is that they can be used so well in the ornamental landscape design around a house. A woody food-bearing plant can be directly substituted for a similar ornamental. For example, a flowering cherry offers nothing but flowers while a fruiting cherry blooms

Small-Budget Buy

The most valuable plants to the budget gardener are those that offer two values in one plant. These two-for-one plants are your best buy no matter what the purchase price because of their expanded value. If you pay $20 for a hedge shrub, you can buy a blueberry and use it as a hedge for the same price. But, you'll get blueberries also! Whenever you buy a plant with this second value, whether it's cut flowers, food, decorating material, healing medicine, fragrance, or other useful qualities, it is twice as valuable. These plants allow you to literally create twice the garden.

Fruiting strawberries can be highly ornamental when grown in pots.

Catalog and Online Sources for Fruits, Veggies, and Herbs

Baker Creek Heirloom Seeds; Big John's Garden; Brown's Omaha Plant Farms, Inc.; Burgess Seed and Plant Co.; Dixondale Farms; Dominion Seed House (Canada); Doyle's Thornless Blackberry, Inc.; Farmer Seed and Nursery; Field & Forest Products; Garden Crossings; Gro 'N Sell, Inc.; Gurney's Seed and Nursery Co.; House of Wesley, Inc.; Indiana Berry & Plant Co.; Irish Eyes – Garden City Seeds; J.E. Miller Nurseries; Native Seeds/SEARCH; One Green World; Raintree Nurseries; Seeds of Change; Stark Bros. Nurseries and Orchards Co.; The Pepper Gal; Willhite Seed Co.; Woodprairie Farm.

Seed companies like Burpee have produced new catalogs each year for over a century. Please check out Chapter 6 for the web addresses of these companies.

just as heavily followed by a fabulous crop of fruit. The key to using woody plants is to avoid sequestering them in a food garden but to use them as substitutes for purely ornamental landscape plants.

Tightwad Gardening Tip

If your ground is hard, try soaking it with a sprinkler to make it softer before you start turning it over. Do this at least 24 hours in advance because newly wet ground can be sticky and muddy. You want the ground moist, not wet, before you go to work.

The $30 Tomato

Don't make the mistake of spending more on growing food in your garden than you would buying produce. It happens every day! Too often folks become enamored with raised beds and complex ideas when they are standing on perfectly good soil for a garden. Unless your garden site is solid clay or all rocks, you can grow plants there. The only thing you need to get started is a good load of organic matter to enrich the biotic activity. There are dozens of places you can obtain organic matter in the form of manure, compost, and leaf mold for incredibly low prices or free. Refer to Chapter 3 for sources and ideas as well as details on low-cost organic soil improvements.

If you are starting small, invest in a good spading fork and start turning that ground. It's hard work but great exercise too, and more productive than lifting weights at the gym where you have to pay *them!* Once you rough till, spread the organic matter and turn it again, breaking up the clods into a finer and finer texture. Then rake the surface smooth while removing roots, sticks, rocks, and other debris. Once the ground is clean, *voila*, you're ready to plant. Compare that with the cost of wood and hardware and footings and buying and trucking all that extra dirt to create a raised bed and see how simple gardening really is. It's the people that sell all that stuff who like to make it more complicated.

If you decide to create a larger garden, you might want to spend the money to rent a tiller for a day. This is the biggest expense you'll have and it will pay off on a larger, more productive food garden. Resist buying a tiller that will have to be maintained each year because that cost takes forever to recoup. Plus, it's easier to have the rental yard mechanic help you get a recalcitrant tiller running again.

Critter Fence

If you have pets, chances are they'll dig in your garden. It's natural for them to want to play in all that finely tilled ground. A dog can destroy your freshly planted garden overnight. Worse yet are rabbits that may nibble it down to nubs in the same length of time. This is an age-old problem that has traditionally been solved with the picket fence. Closely spaced pickets are too narrow to allow rabbits to squeeze their way in. Another critter to watch out for are chickens; chickens can really damage a young garden. Fortunately they aren't great fliers and may not be willing to fly over a picket fence, but they have been known to fly up onto fencing, and then jump off the other side. That is why pickets are traditionally pointed to keep chickens from perching there, thus discouraging them from entering the garden.

Whether it's a dog or wild rabbits, you'll need to construct a fence for the lowest price possible. The best material is steel

Top Free Food Plant Catalogs and Toll-Free Numbers
Burpee – The most well-known and beloved seed seller. (800) 888-1447
Johnny's Selected Seeds – Geared for market gardeners. (877) 564-6697
Jung Seeds & Plants – Offers great diversity and supplies. (800) 247-5864
Seeds of Change – Has a wide range of heirloom varieties. (888) 762-7333
Stark Brothers Nurseries – Offers fruit trees and berries. (800) 325-4180

T-posts used for wire livestock fencing, which is often sold as field fence or hog wire. Wire fences feature a smaller mesh near the bottom of the fencing, which discourages small animals from entering. But if it is not small enough to keep rabbits out, be prepared to line the fence with a two-foot wide strip of chicken wire to keep the garden critter free.

Assign a Compost Area

It's far more convenient to designate an area within your veggie garden to create a compost pile. For most folks, a compost bin may be made out of recycled materials and it won't be that attractive—but it will be functional.

If there's a fence around the garden plot, you can rest assured the compost is going to be safe from kids and pets, too. If it draws a few flies or has an occasional odor, locating it in the garden won't be as much of a problem. (Although the areas where compost does its job by decomposing aren't supposed to draw flies or have an odor, this is an inexact science, particularly for beginners.) Finally, if you have a big compost heap, you won't have to drag it so far to enrich your garden soil.

When Raised Beds Are A Must

Though they are more work initially and potentially costly to set up, raised beds can be great problem solvers for problem home-sites. In situations where the planting site has very poor soil or there is hardpan or a dozen other issues, raised beds get you gardening quickly.

Do not underestimate how much it may cost to build raised beds. The traditional way uses wood 4x4 posts on the corners anchored in concrete footings and connected by long sideboards. The footing is labor intensive and the connections are very important to maintain structural integrity. To create a project of any size it can get very pricey for wood, hardware, and obtaining the

This large compost bin was made of surplus wood shipping pallets attached at the corners.

tools you need to get the job done. But ultimately, you may be able to grow more in less space, with less work, and use fewer resources—because you are also creating the garden site to be in a perfect form.

Keep in mind that your cost to make raised beds will be offset by the way you use them. Rather than the traditional garden row layout, which originated from large rural gardens using flood irrigation, raised beds better lend themselves to a different way of gardening. Its roots are in the way the Pueblo tribes created waffle-style gardens in the Desert Southwest. The concept was

expanded upon by respected authority Mel Bartholomew, who showed America how to apply this same water- and space-conserving technique in his book *All New Square Foot Gardening*. Though you may have more upfront cost for raised beds, the increased yield will pay you back in just a few seasons.

Building a raised bed is a big project that can prove daunting for those without the time, skills, or tools to create

This simple, three-tier raised bed illustrates how composite lumber and corner fittings can result in a foundation-free raised bed.

them from scratch. Plus, despite the fact that redwood and cedar resist decomposition, they are not rot-proof, particularly with this much wood in contact with soil. Some gardeners use pressure-treated lumber impregnated with very powerful chemicals. Though it is less expensive than redwood, the chemicals may prove unacceptable to strict organic gardeners. Finally, be aware that the soil within a raised bed can become very heavy when it's saturated. Many types of soil can expand considerably when they get wet, adding further pressure on the sideboards.

Green Choices

Lumber created out of recycled plastics is an exceptional product for use in gardens because it won't rot like wood does. Yet it is manufactured in standard lumber sizes so you can use it as a substitute for wood in any project such as raised beds. When you utilize this composite lumber you are supporting massive recycling and at the same time reducing dependence on forest products.

One way to reduce costs and simplify raised bed construction is to use corner connectors. These are metal or plastic corner brackets designed to fit a standard board such as 2x6 or 2x8, the sizes that are usually used for raised bed sideboards. Corner connectors can be purchased in three different designs. The rigid 90-degree corner is made of painted metal, looks great, and offers the best structural integrity for beds of larger sizes. Hinged corners, typically made of plastic, allow you do create beds of nearly every shape. This can be vital for tight spaces where a standard square or rectangle won't fit. It also helps to maximize the area where you can garden because the option to build an unusual shape may pick up a few extra square feet. Buy six hinged corners to make a beautiful, hexagonal garden or just three to make a corner triangle raised bed. Stackable corners are designed to allow you greater depth within your raised beds. Simply cut two or three sets of identical sideboards. Set the bottom row, then the next, and then the third for up to two feet of depth. This kind of corner, when combined with recycled plastic lumber, makes the best raised bed of all.

What makes corners so good is that once the entire bed is fitted together, there is no need for corner posts and footings. A rectangle shape is naturally able to support itself over any surface whether it's rocky ground, impervious adobe clay, or even a concrete slab. So if you're a city dweller and have nothing but

a concrete backyard, you can use this system to create a raised bed despite the lack of earth! This method saves money and labor, plus you can use old recycled lumber without concerns that it won't hold up under traditional corner fastening methods.

In the past folks made raised beds out of anything they could get inexpensively or free. This resulted in some unique gardens, but many of them were not particularly attractive. But when food gardening is the goal, aesthetics are not your primary concern—productivity is. Here are some options for creating raised beds using often discarded or recycled materials:

Corner fittings that are made like a hinge allow the raised bed to take on any shape.

Concrete Block: Ordinary two-cell concrete block makes a great raised bed, but only to a depth of 8 to 10 inches. Lay the blocks out end to end and then fill the cells with soil, gravel or any fine materials you have on hand. Because there is no anchorage nor are the blocks connected to one another, they are easily pushed out of place as soil expands and contracts. Pound a stake into all or every few blocks to give them more stability.

Railroad Ties: Railroad ties are a longstanding raised bed building component because these beams are so large and heavy they stay in place all by themselves. A single level can be over a foot deep if the tie is laid on its short side. To have more than a single layer, stack them by offsetting the seams, just as brick

Easy-Grow Potatoes

Over the years folks have dreamed up all sorts of solutions for growing where there is no natural soil. This method is excellent for growing gourmet fingerling potatoes. This older technique utilizes burlap bags filled with potting soil. The bag is filled with soil, then sewn closed at the top. Set the bag on its side and cut a few small holes evenly spaced through the top. Plant a seed potato in the soil through the hole you cut. Keep the soil moist and your potatoes will grow beautifully provided they are kept evenly moist. When it's time to harvest just cut open the bag and harvest the potatoes.

Since burlap bags or gunnysacks aren't that common anymore, a better alternative has taken their place. Bags for animal feed and bulk foods are now made of durable woven plastic so they breathe just like burlap, but are less prone to decomposition. You can plant an entire season's garden inside these plastic bags, standing them on end against a wall or laying them down to produce other forms of veggies. A good place to obtain these bags free is at feed stores, farms and ranches with livestock, breweries, and anywhere else bulk materials are shipped in sacks.

is laid. To give the bed more integrity, drill a hole down through the wood with a very long drill bit. Then pound old pipe or rebar through the hole to at least six inches into native soil. This will effectively hold the levels together.

Concrete Fragments: You can stack any flat material whether it's stone, concrete fragments, or steppingstones to create height. This is an attractive alternative particularly if it is adjacent to an existing block wall so it has something solid to lean on. Although they are time consuming and very heavy to haul, this kind of masonry should, hopefully, originate on-site.

Soil for Raised Beds

One of the biggest challenges of raised beds is obtaining quality topsoil to fill them. If it's a smaller project, you can use bagged materials, but once you start filling the beds you'll understand just how much soil it takes.

Inexpensive or Free Soil Sources

Buying topsoil by the cubic yard can be expensive. Yet every day there are companies excavating soil that must pay someone to take a load of dirt away or find a suitable fill site. Give a call to these companies because they often excavate footings, basements, and pools, as well as irrigation ditches and ponds. However, be aware that soil obtained from someone else's poor ground will be just as poor in your garden. Ask questions about where the soil comes from and whether it is topsoil, less fertile subsoil, or a mixture of both. You must also have a location prepared for it to be dumped while you transport it into your beds. Be prepared to have your driveway occupied by dirt, so lay out some tarps or plastic ahead of time.

Some potential phone book or Internet sources of excavated soil include: Swimming Pool Contractor, General Contractor, Excavating Engineers, Aggregate Company, Farmer, and Rancher.

Ways to Save in the Garden

The key to a low-cost veggie or kitchen garden is to avoid falling for all the smaller products for sale everywhere from the grocery store to garden center. If you think you need it, ask yourself if the pioneers had that, and if not, *maybe* it's not necessary. Don't forget they grew enormous gardens using what they had at hand, and so can you. This is where most folks get into trouble—thinking they need to buy things they can make or do without quite nicely.

This garden features wire fence cages to protect individual plants and an upside down L deer fence that is cantilevered so it is too wide for deer to leap over.

Straw Bale Mulch

The vegetable garden always grows better when it's mulched. A layer of mulch on the surface of the soil keeps moisture in, shades the root zone for cooler conditions, and discourages weed growth. Without question the least expensive way to mulch both plants and aisles of a garden is with straw. For smaller gardens or raised beds you may choose something else, but when it comes to the in-ground sizeable plot, there's no substitute for straw for price and function.

Indian corn purchased the first year to decorate your home can be planted the following spring to yield a new crop of similar ear size and kernel color.

Trellis and Tepee

When you have plants that climb, you need a support structure. One of the most common for pole beans is the tepee style. Using long sticks held together at the top allows you to plant at the base of each tepee for a perfect support.

This technique may be expanded in a variety of different ways. If the support is created pup-tent style you can lay netting over the form to give peas a fine mesh to climb. You can also lay wire fence or chicken wire against the surface and tie it in place with wire.

Green Choices

If you feel bad about all the Christmas trees thrown out each year, those with a wood "X" nailed to the bottom can become freestanding pea trellises. Simply bury the bottom "X" in the soil and plant your peas around it. As the season progresses you'll have a beautiful, conical pea tower. This is a good reason to hijack a neighbor's January cast-off Christmas tree for a great reuse in June!

Deer Fencing

Deer can be the most discouraging part of gardening in American suburbs. They will eat virtually everything you plant if the plot is not fenced. The problem is that deer are high jumpers and therefore you must create a *really* tall fence, which is expensive *and* ugly. One option is to use tree branches to extend the height of your existing fence, then wrap it all in fine tree netting used to keep birds out of fruit. The deer feel this with their noses but it's so finely textured you hardly see it from a distance.

Another option is a strategy fence based on the fact that deer aren't long jumpers. If your fence can be made wider, the deer won't jump it. One technique is to make your fence in an upside down L shape. The cantilevered part should extend three to four feet. Another option is to create two fences, four feet apart. Though these are space-consuming alternatives, they are quite functional and free your yard from the high-security prison look!

And More Ways to Save in the Garden

Wire Twist Ties: Use these to attach tomato vines and other climbers to their support structures.

Newspaper: Place a few sections folded together beneath gourds, melons, and winter squash to keep them separate from muddy ground, bugs, and bacteria.

Tool Locker: Dedicate an old ice chest to become a tool locker in your garden where you can store your hand tools, supplies, and leftover seeds so you won't have to carry them back to the house.

This simple pea or bean trellis is constructed of tree stakes connected by welded wire panels designed to reinforce concrete slabs. To the right, an old wood market umbrella skeleton serves as a secondary home for climbers.

Whether you have six supports or ten, the garden tepee is an old-time favorite for pole beans.

Gourds are a perfect crop to train onto your fences.

Grow More Décor

Your vegetable garden can grow more than just food crops. There are some really fun plants to add that offer unique decorating and crafting options. These give you and your family a natural opportunity to become creative with plants that are useful, historic, and very easy to grow.

Gourds are left in the field to dry, then are cured over winter, and finally the seeds are removed after they're fully dried, which is when decorating begins.

Plant Indian Corn

Every year we buy colorful Indian corn for the holidays and then toss it out. But did you know that these forms of early corn and popcorn are really viable seed? If you love those little strawberry-colored corn with the ruby kernels, grow a patch of them from the seed of a single cob. Or if you're into any of the other colors you find, grow a patch and at harvest time you'll be able to enjoy your own homegrown decorations.

Grow Gourds for Gifts and Pots

Humans stored their food and drink in gourds long before the invention of pottery. In fact, the earliest forms of pottery were actually modeled after the useful shapes of bottle gourds. These are as easy and inexpensive to grow from seed as winter squash, and they make a fine crop to grow alongside a fence to keep the large vines out of the way. Grow gourds from quality seed and discover how to cure and decorate them for beautiful fall arrangements or beautifully detailed pots that make fabulous, free gifts.

Broom Corn

Broom corn is related to sorghum but it looks a lot like a corn stalk. Its large and very hard seeds are borne at the top of the plant. Pioneers grew broom corn in America to create high quality sweeping brooms, which are demonstrated to this day in living history exhibits all over the eastern states. Grow your own broom corn to feed wild birds in the fall, to cut for indoor arrangements, or to make your own old-fashioned looking brooms to display on a porch or patio.

To make brooms the seed is removed, but if broom corn is left as it is, the dried sprigs can be left around the garden for winter birds.

Broom corn is an early American crop cultivated to create straw brooms.

11 Your Tax Dollars at Work:
Government payoffs.

"Cultivators of the earth are the most valuable citizens. They are the most vigorous, the most independent, the most virtuous, and they are tied to their country and wedded to its liberty and interests by the most lasting bands."
— Thomas Jefferson

Government, from the federal level down to your city offices, is a massive resource your taxes have supported over the years. Its agencies and interests have produced an incredible amount of information, and now much of it is available online, just a few clicks away. Previously you had to send for printed materials; not only are they now available online, they usually have much better color photography or illustrations and they are kept up to date. Plus, the databases of cultivated and wild plants provide the most accurate information you can find on subjects from the latest diseases of trees to lists of potentially invasive plants.

United States Department of Agriculture

The USDA has undergone a huge revamping that combined many departments under its care. Dozens of agencies have been renamed to expand their areas of interest or to better focus on twenty-first-century issues. For example, the Soil Conservation Service, which was first created to prevent another Dust Bowl, focused previously on more protective means of caring for agricultural soils and preventing erosion. Today it's been renamed the National Resources Conservation Service and covers similar issues plus many others relating to habitat preservation and restoration.

These agencies have created a huge number of online publications you can access, download, and print if you wish. Finding information with-out printing it is a greener choice because it will always be there to refer to time and again without using forest byproducts.

This website—www.usda.gov— is the portal to all things gathered beneath the USDA umbrella. If you click on the "Browse By Audience" option in the left bar, select "Consumer." This turns all the options to the many materials and databases suitable to regular homeowners. There's a section that helps you find local farmers' markets in your area. In the center, click on "Homeowners, Urban and Suburban Land Users" to access many excellent and accurate publications on wildlife and ways to conserve the environment through your backyard garden. On the right side click on "Gardening" to access even more useful data and links on these important subjects:

When drought struck in the early twentieth century after the protective layers of prairie sod had been stripped away by the plow, there was nothing to keep the soil from blowing away.

Agricultural extension offices across America (which offer locally specific assistance)
Home and Garden Information Center
Home Gardening Tips
National Agricultural Library's Gardening Resources
National Arboretum Gardening Tips
Organic Vegetable Gardens
Plant Hardiness Zones

Click on "Plant Health" and you'll access one of the most complete resources for pests and diseases in the world. This well-illustrated and very detailed resource is an archive of articles, photos, and publications that will tell you virtually everything you need to know about garden pests.

PLANTS Database

The PLANTS site (http://plants.usda.gov) is the primary plant database for the United States government. It can be searched by plant name or by other criteria; for example, you can ask it to provide a list of plants that are native to your state. Each plant profile displays a map of the locations where the plants are native or where they have naturalized in the United States.

There are many excellent reference links that connect you to other databases such as those focusing on Native American food plants, medicine, or insect data. The PLANTS database has many photos of profiled plants to give you an idea of how they look at various stages of growth or in different regions. If you need to know whether a plant is potentially invasive in your state or region, this is the site where the world meets to assess these kinds of potential threats to native vegetation.

The Benefits of Local Government

Some of the best and most accurate gardening information can be obtained through state resources. Among these is the Master Gardener program designed to assist home gardeners. This program educates and trains volunteers who must eventually give back in the form of several hours of service in exchange for their education. The Master Gardener program is a great resource that makes it possible for a knowledgeable gardener to come out to your house for any large or vexing problems.

Topsoil losses during the Dust Bowl were so great the Soil Conservation Service was created to help farmers develop better ways to protect the land against the ravages of erosion.

Master Gardeners work with the University Agricultural Extension system, which has offices across America. These resources are good to know if you decide to make some major improvements such as planting a woodlot, or siting a family

garden, or installing a home vineyard. Visit or call the Ag Extension office before attempting a large project to obtain the best advice possible, particularly since the offices (hence, advice) are regionally specific.

Few citizens realize their city and county governments prepare detailed guidelines for development and that many of these include local landscaping ordinances. These are often lists of trees and shrubs believed to do well under urban conditions without any serious problems such as litter or invasive rooting. This data is often found under the Department of Public Works, which oversees the trees approved for planting along streets and boulevards. These same lists will give you the best choices for planting at your home, too, if you are interested in the same criteria. You may also find literature on water conservation, passive solar planting design, and a variety of other important subjects of interest to the local community.

Utility Companies

Your electric power and natural-gas supplies may be provided from your local government or private companies. Many of these companies or government agencies have ongoing programs that help educate the public on ways to reduce energy consumption and ways landscaping influences the microclimates around your home. You may be surprised at the amount of detail on tree selection, location, and planting techniques.

In the West, water conservation is among the most vital problems facing communities. Many water resource entities, whether they are government or private, strongly support helping consumers landscape for water conservation. Water agencies on all levels produce many kinds of literature that are very helpful and often have conservation "fairs" during which you might even receive a free tree or drought-resistant plant to help you get started on the right foot.

Tree Losses

Every mature tree in your landscape is valuable, a factor recognized by the IRS. If you lose a mature tree to disease or a storm you may lose a lot of landscaping beneath that tree and it's possible your utility bills could increase in summer due to lack of shade. You may be entitled to a tax break or compensation for the loss by your home insurance company. Call your insurance agent and a certified arborist. The arborist will use a standard formula to determine the value of the tree and will provide that in writing, which can be quite helpful later on when negotiating with the IRS or an insurance adjustor. Just as you use photographs to document your household valuables, take photos of your landscape every few years to show its maturity and benefit to the homesite. This will be of great value if you live in regions that suffer earthquakes, wildfire, or floods.

Save More and Live Well

Gardening is more than a hobby; it's a lifestyle. It keeps us close to the earth and offers a great sense of accomplishment when we create something marvelous out of little more than earth, a seed, and water. When money is scarce you are forced to think outside the box to obtain what you once purchased without a second thought. Lack of cash can become the driving force that can transform your life from one focused on store-bought items to an innate consciousness of those things you've ingeniously reused, repurposed, or found for pennies at a yard sale.

This transformation will make you feel good because there's no guilt in small budget gardening. It is a process of creating and tending a garden you'll be intensely proud of because you made it yourself. You didn't just run out and buy everything ready-made. You'll become far more aware of the wayside places around your home and how they might contribute seed and organic matter for home and garden. You'll develop an eye for other people's castoffs and how they can make your planting areas bigger, better, or more beautiful. Above all, your frugal examples will be seen by others who will come to know the monetary value of gardens firsthand.

Small budget gardening can become your legacy; one that can feed you now and for generations to come.

Bibliography

There are many wonderful books filled with great ideas for inexpensive or free gardening, but some are out of print. My library is filled with those I long to share with you but they are no longer widely available. Fortunately, some really great, more recent titles are available that offer much of the same information.

All New Square Foot Gardening
Mel Bartholomew
This must-have for the small space food grower is a detailed manual for getting the most out of your garden or raised beds.
(Cool Springs Press)

The Backyard Homestead
Carleen Madigan (Editor)
The wholistic concept is vital especially during hard financial times. The material inside these pages can lead you down a road of greater self-sufficiency even if you live in the suburbs.
(Storey Publishing)

Backyard Medicine
Julie Bruton-Seal and Matthew Seal
Save money and learn more about common plants that soothe, treat, and cure to cut costs at the drug store.
(Skyhorse Publishing)

Gaia's Garden: A Guide to Home-Scale Permaculture
Toby Hemenway
Permaculture is the most intensive home food production system on earth, and this book is packed with great ideas and tips on how to combine plants to optimize harvest.
(Chelsea Green Publishing)

Lowes Creative Ideas for Outdoor Living
This softcover book is packed with great ideas for using paint and found or repurposed objects to make your garden visually exciting for pennies.

Making More Plants
Ken Druse
This is the best how-to book on plant propagation from seed
to grafting and everything else you need to know presented in
exquisitely clear photography and instructive text.
(Clarkson Potter)

The Mother Earth News Almanac
Originally published in 1973, this pocket paperback contains the
greatest ideas of the 1970s issues of *Mother Earth News*, the
original alternative lifestyle magazine that is just as timely today.
(Bantam Books)

Reinvent Your Garden
In the traditional Sunset how-to style, you'll be inspired to
expand or upgrade your garden with low-cost DIY projects and
spectacular plants. (Sunset)

Rodale Organic Gardening Solutions
Cheryl Long and the Editors of Organic Gardening Magazine
This great little book is packed with fabulous ideas for solv-
ing problems without spending money on expensive products.
(Rodale Press)

The Urban Homestead
Kelly Coyne and Erik Knutzen
Written by a couple transforming their downtown Los Angeles
homesite into a highly productive urban farm.
(Process Self Reliance)

Vegetables, Herbs and Fruit: An Illustrated Encyclopedia
Matthew Biggs, Jekka McVicar, and Bob Flowerdew
For the new food gardener, this thick reference book is incredibly
helpful for getting you oriented toward food plants of all kinds
and how to get started growing and cooking with them.
(Firefly Books)

Seasonal Gardening Notes

SPRING

SUMMER

FALL

WINTER

Meet Mo

Maureen "Mo" Gilmer is counted among the top garden communicators in America. As an author and photographer, she has authored more than seventeen books on gardening, landscape design, and the environment, and is a freelance writer and photographer for many industry and consumer magazines.

Gilmer's media appearances include *The View*, *The Early Show*, and *Good Morning America* as well as countless demonstration segments for network news affiliates. Gilmer was host, project designer, and coproducer of *Weekend Gardening*, a weekly show that aired on the Scripps DIY Network. Her national weekly column "Yardsmart" is syndicated by Scripps Howard News Service and United Media and is in its fifth year of syndication.

Gilmer has also been associated with industry leaders, including acting as a consultant, working with Monrovia, writing catalogs and brochures, and creating lectures for garden shows. Currently she is Database Editor for *Learn2Grow*.

Her newest books include *Palm Springs-Style Gardening*, which offers the first truly design-oriented book for dry Southwestern climates using both native and exotic plants, and *The Small Budget Gardener*, her first book with Cool Springs Press.

Maureen lives in central Palm Springs with her husband, Jim. When not working, she is usually found at the stable or riding her Quarter Horse.